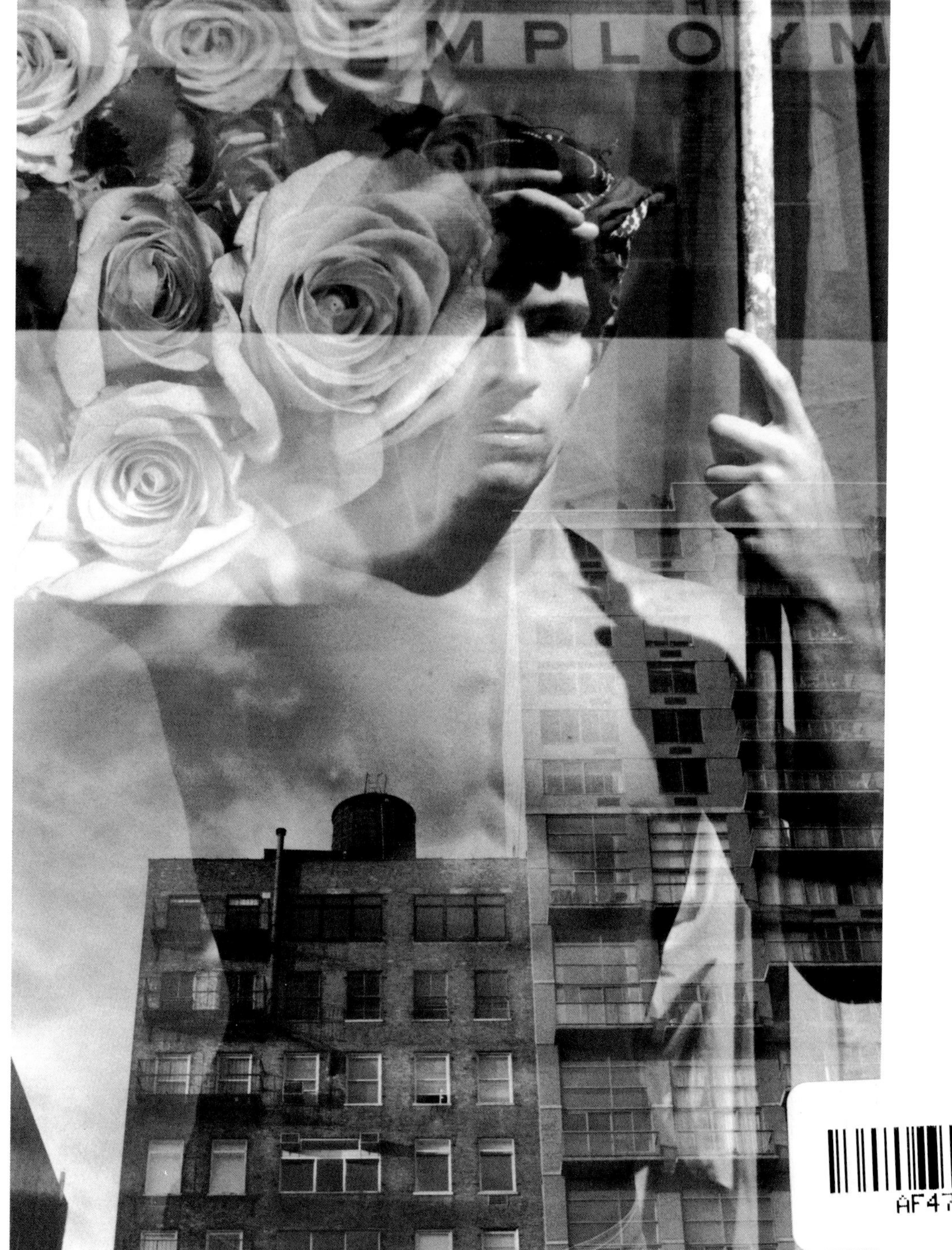
MPLOYM

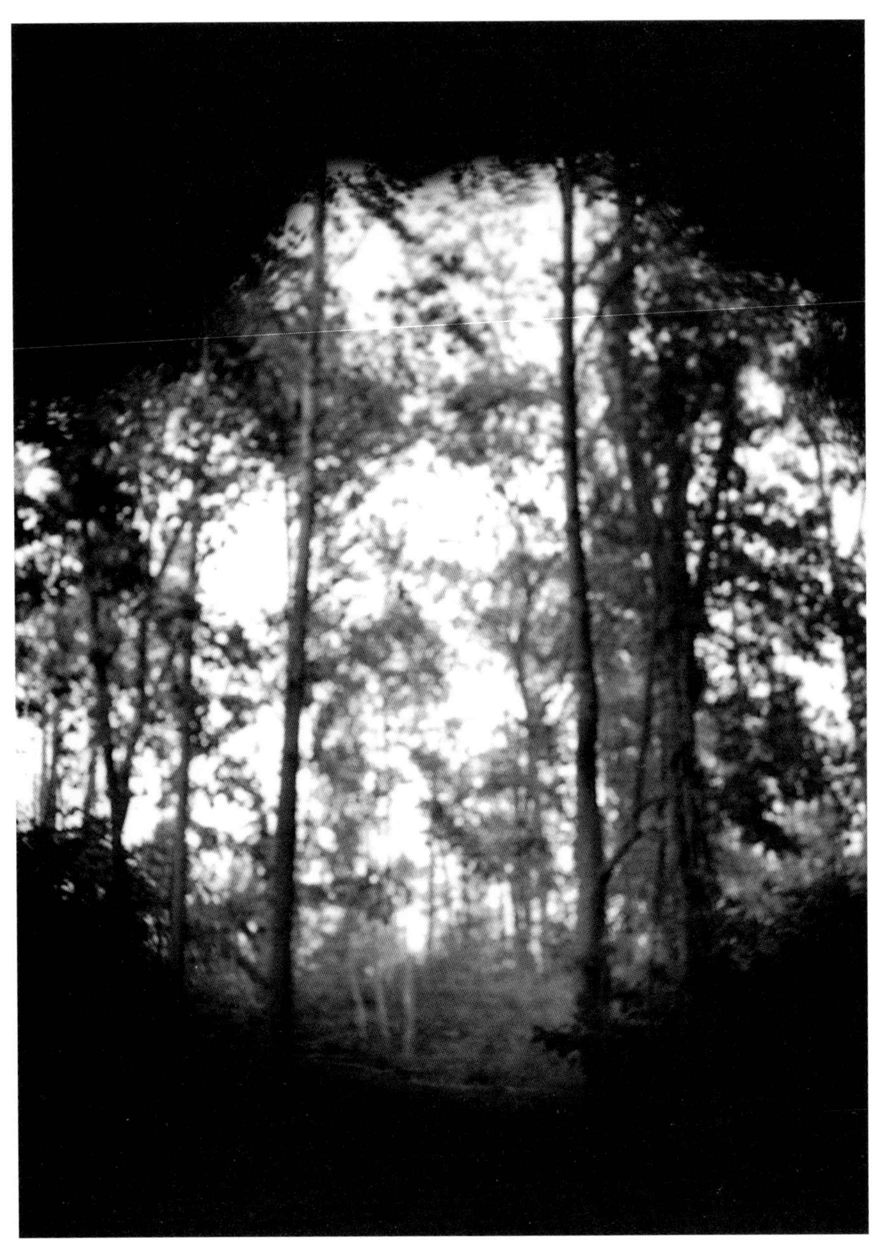

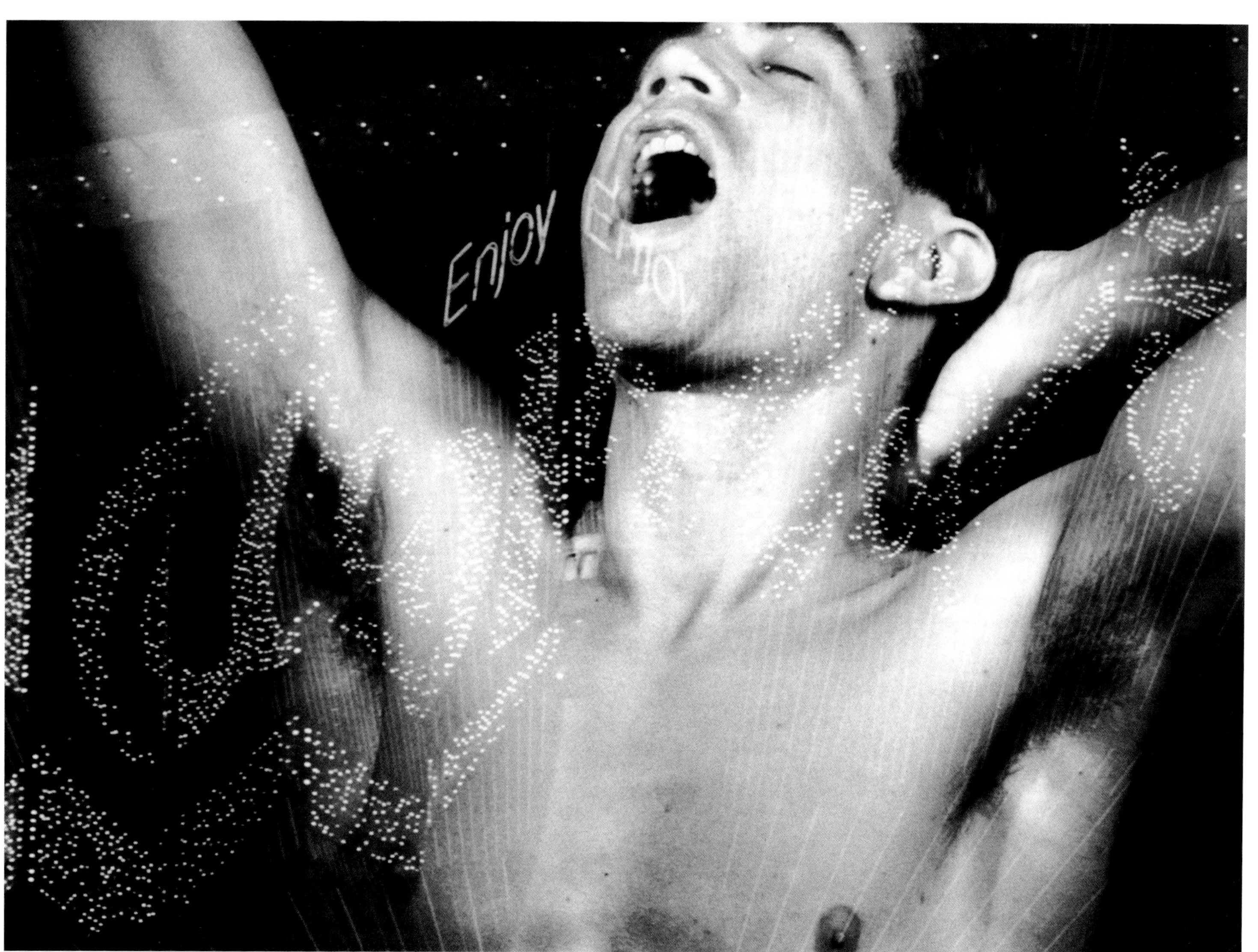
Enjoy

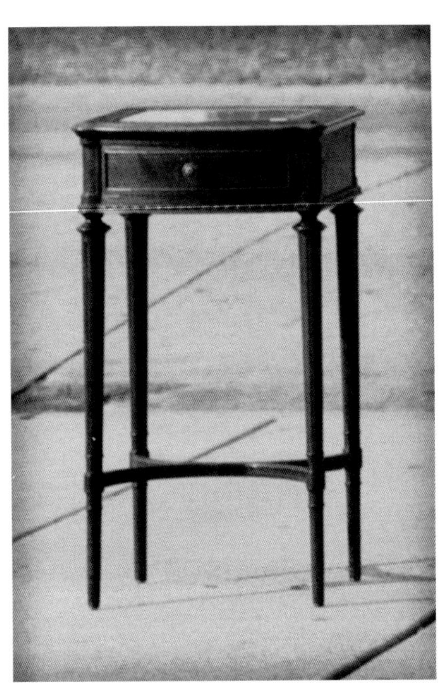

shutter goes
    you're taken
petals shower
bricks come down
a mix of mortar
city wailing
    wordless
fast the flower's taken
streaming light
a body's shape
endows your eyes with rain
I'm sure now that I know you
hold you in a darkened room
a limestone shade you've taken on
keenly made
    and true
my heart's unwitting likeness
now are you

B.T.

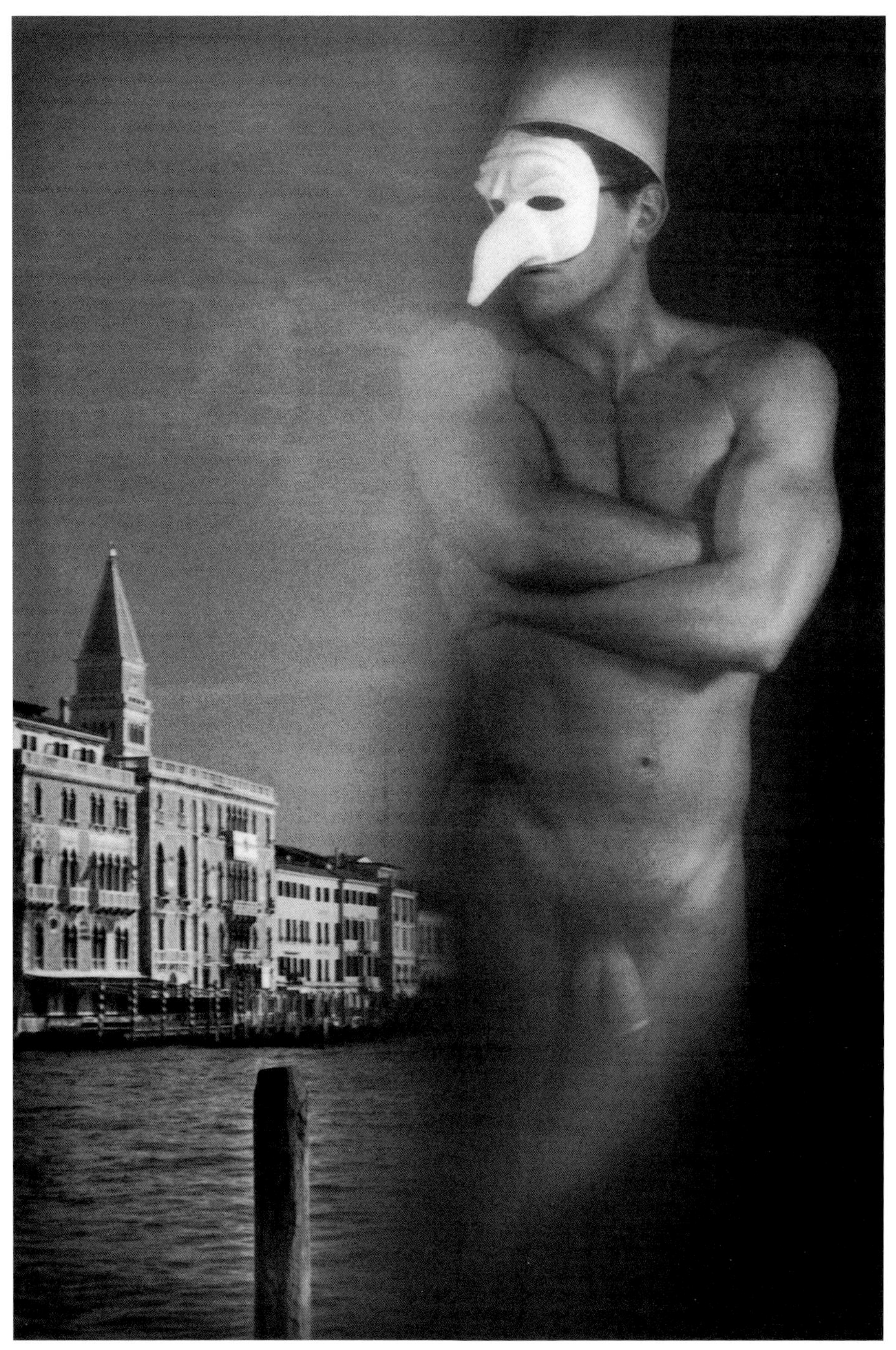

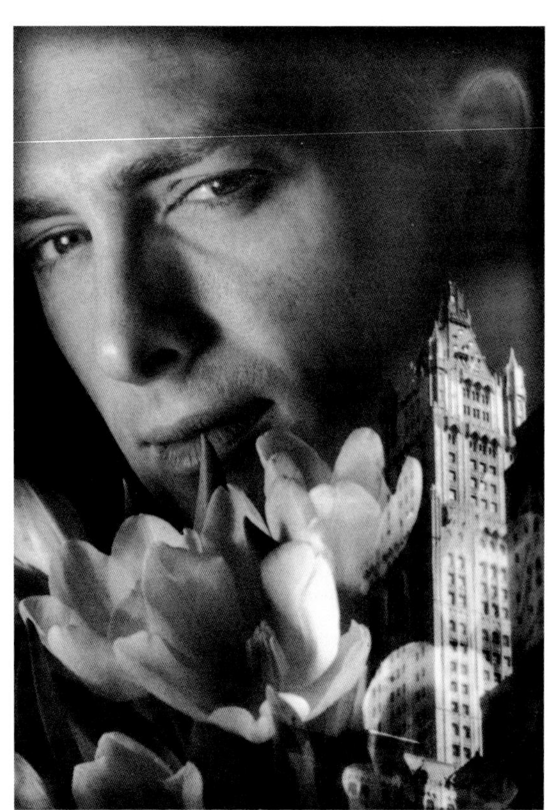

HEART'S
unwitting
LIKENESS

BRIAN
THEIS

HEART'S

unwitting

LIKENESS

BRIAN

THEIS

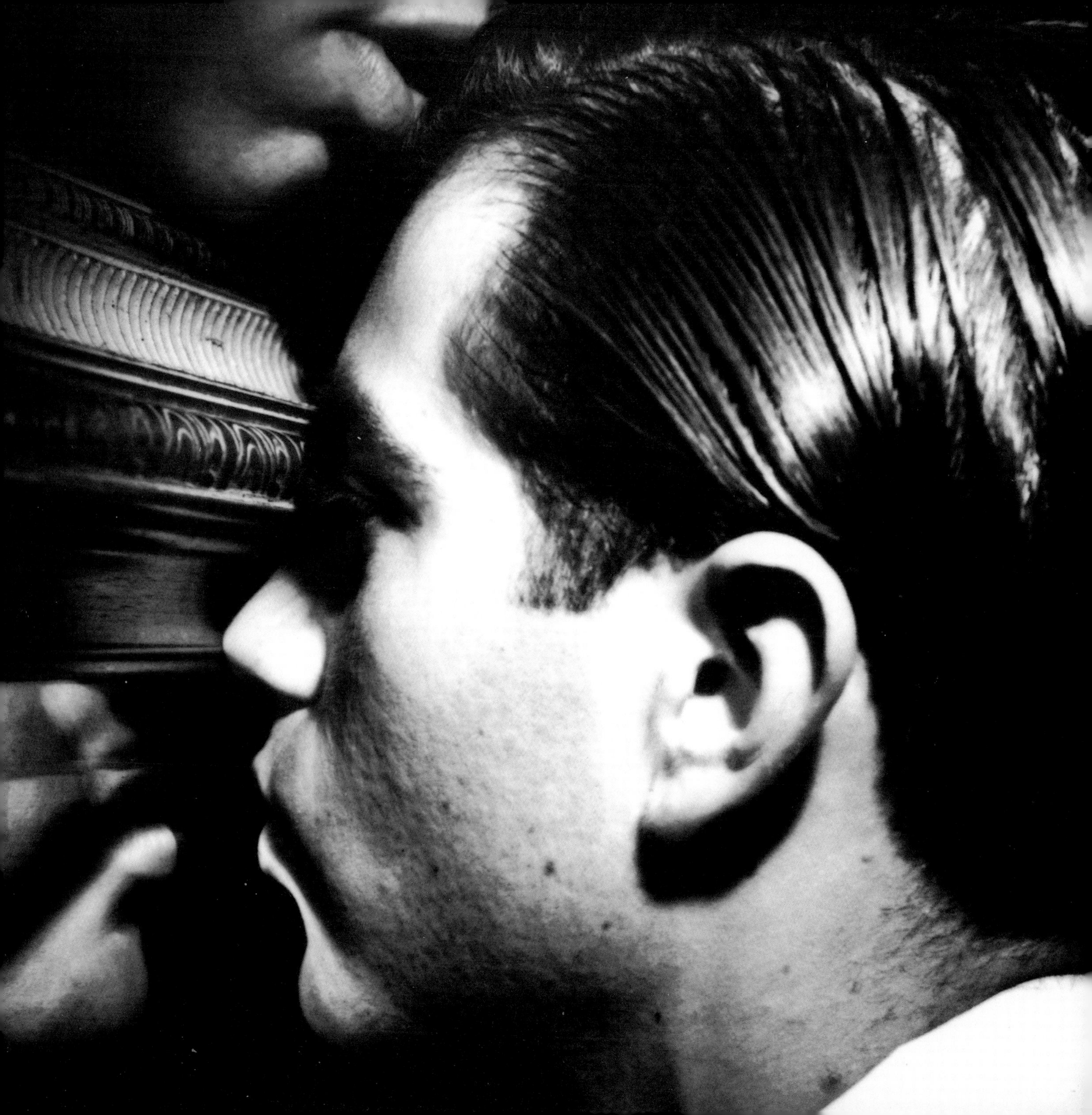

Designed by Robert S. Keefe
Printed by Fred Weidner & Son Printers Inc., New York, N.Y.

ISBN 0-9667130-0-1

"I Went," "Morning Sea," "Ionic," "Tomb of Iasis," and "In Evening" by C. P. Cavafy.
Translations © Daniel Mendelsohn. Printed by permission.

Publicity: Clifford Public Relations, New York.
French title translations: Wendy Murdock.
Women's hair: Charles Ward.
Makeup for Lypsinka and Russell Lewis: Paddy Crofton, The Make-up Shop, NYC.
Pulcinella costume: Steve Epstein.
Assistant to the photographer: Dean Denmon.

Accolades to: Cortland Jessup, Charles Cowles, Race Willard, John Epperson,
Sally Mann, Randal Kleiser, and all of the benevolent collectors and gifted models
without whose good spirit this book would not exist.

Lamia Ink! is an arts organization. An instigator of dialogue between and amongst cultures, genders, generations, and media in alternative formats/forums in both urban and remote areas, producing, promoting and nurturing through performance, publications, and exhibitions. Since 1990.

This edition limited to 1000 copies.

Thus conscience doth make cowards of us all,
                                    –*Hamlet,* III. i.

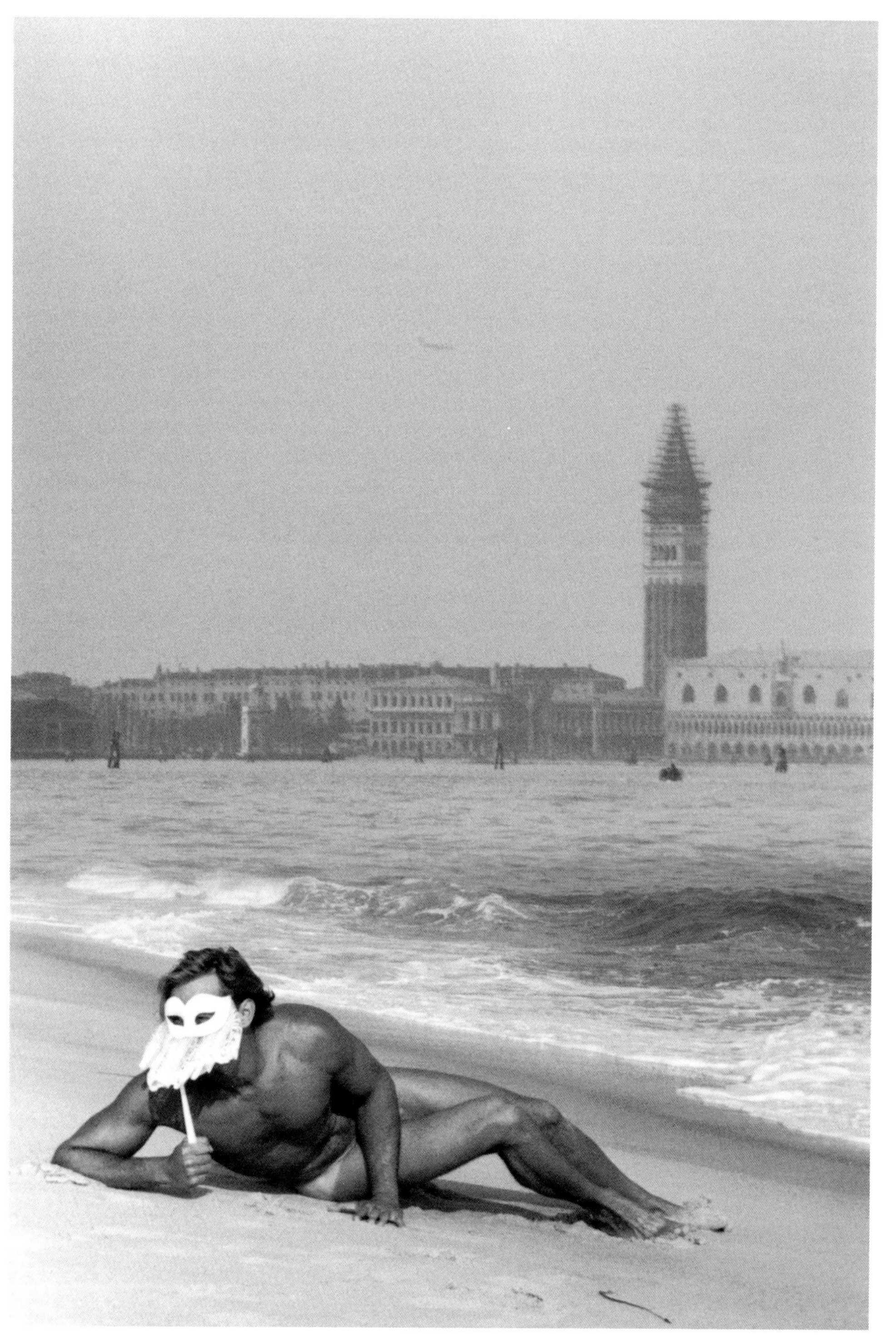

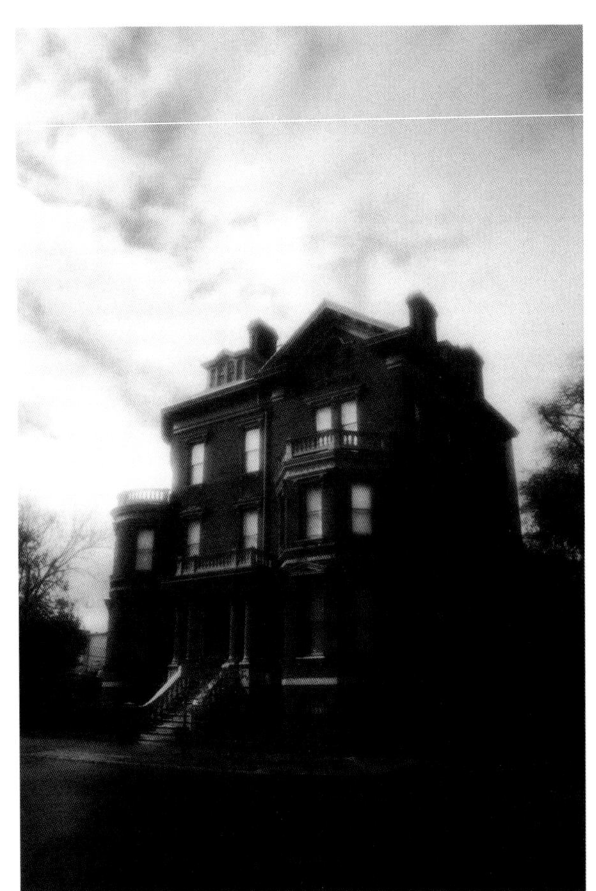

INTRODUCTION

Charles Cowles

The work of Brian Theis is difficult to analyze during this era of cynicism in contemporary art. There is a romantic formalism and emotional sincerity reminiscent of the past. He seeks identity, while seeming to comment on the history of photography time and again.

The themes in Theis' work echo ones that recur in exhibitions and collections of twentieth-century photography: cityscapes, signage, still lifes, and figure studies. The dark side of glamour is addressed in these sensuous, urban creations. Longing, ambivalence and solitude are expressed repeatedly by the subjects Brian has thoughtfully chosen.

Influenced by the history of photography, Theis endeavors to reinvigorate the subject matter of his contemporaries with an eye to the past.

Photographers often seem to be at a distinct advantage since the camera is perceived by many to speak the truth. The manipulation and evolution of these personal visions over the course of the twentieth century has occurred at a remarkable pace. Developments have manifested in many ways – multiple exposures, controlled compositions, printing techniques – and are ever-changing as new technologies emerge.

Brian Theis is an energetic and youthful member of this photographic lineage that I would like to introduce you to. I am hopeful that we will see many more glimpses into his vision of reality in the future.

Charles Cowles has assembled a distinguished private collection of photography. He is director of the Charles Cowles Gallery in New York and was the first curator of modern art at the Seattle Art Museum. He began his career as publisher of *Artforum Magazine*.

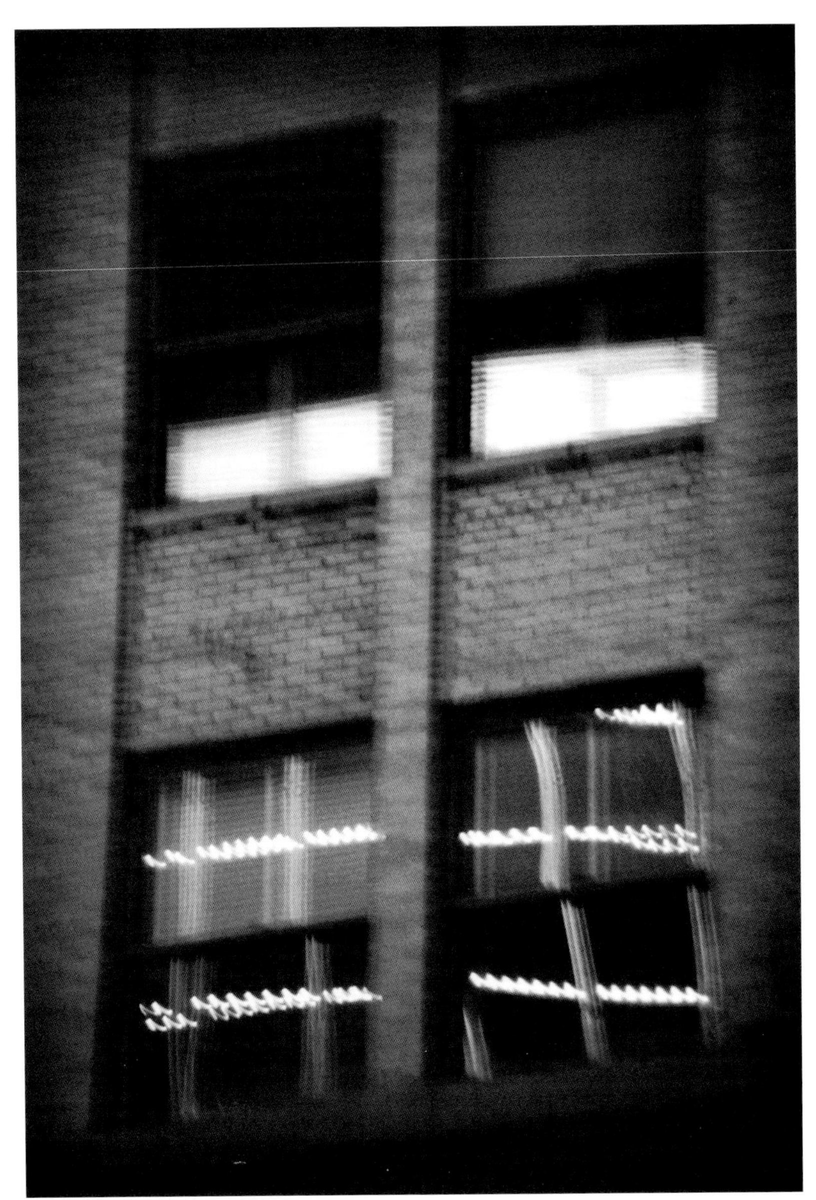

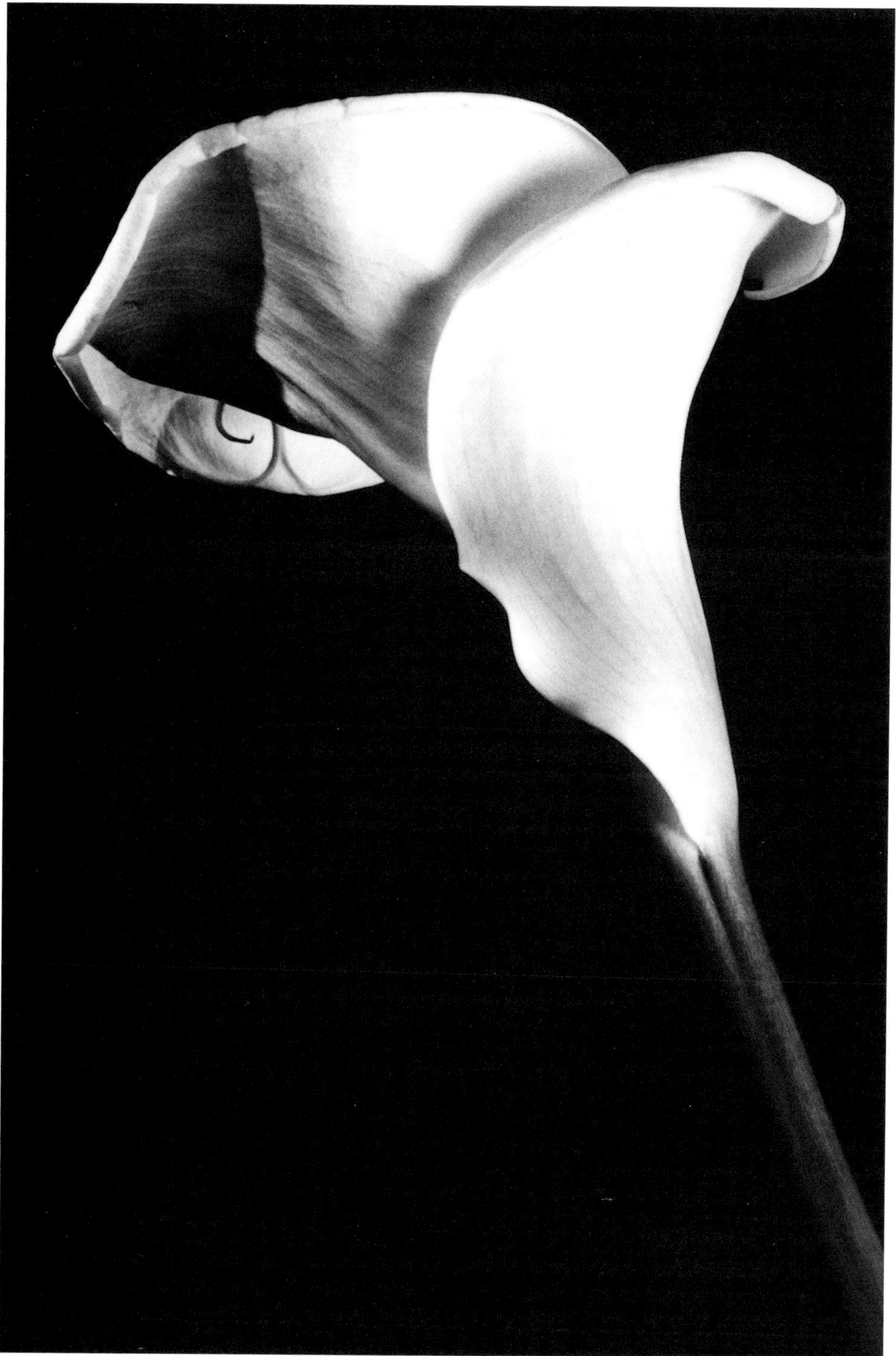

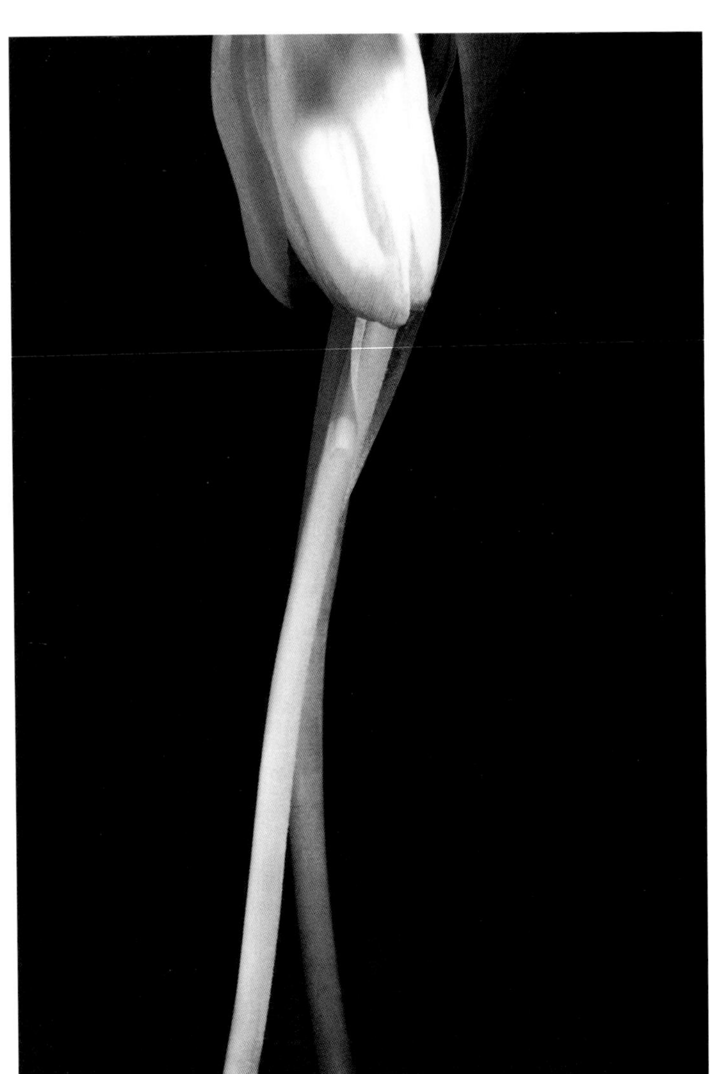

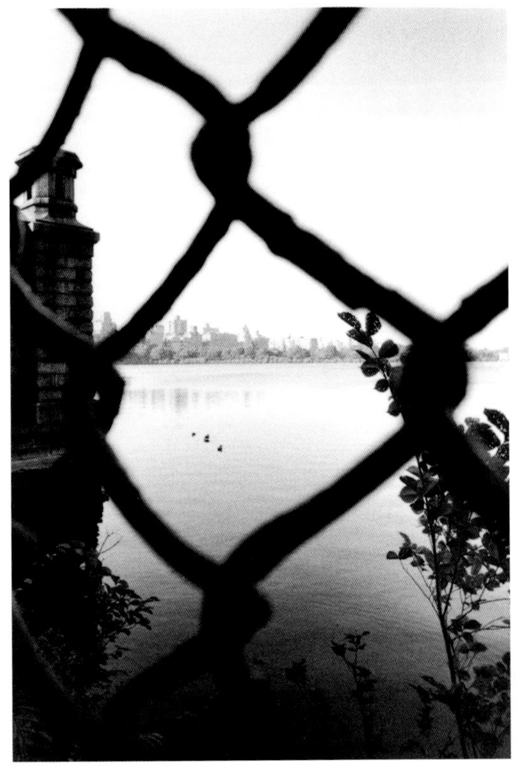

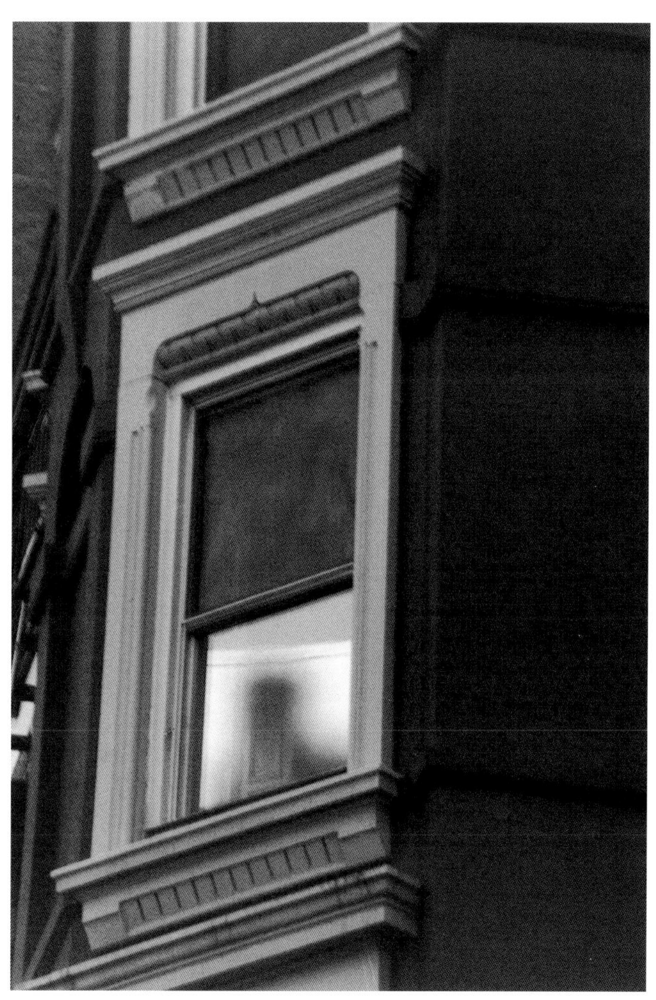

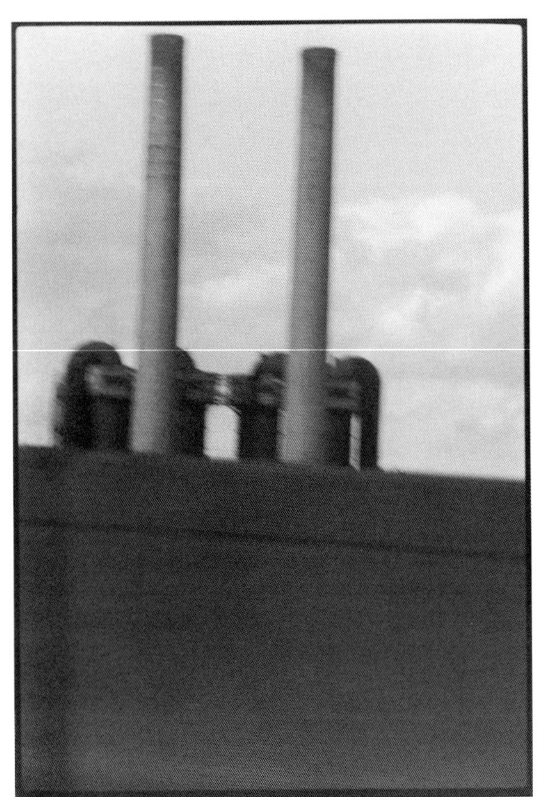

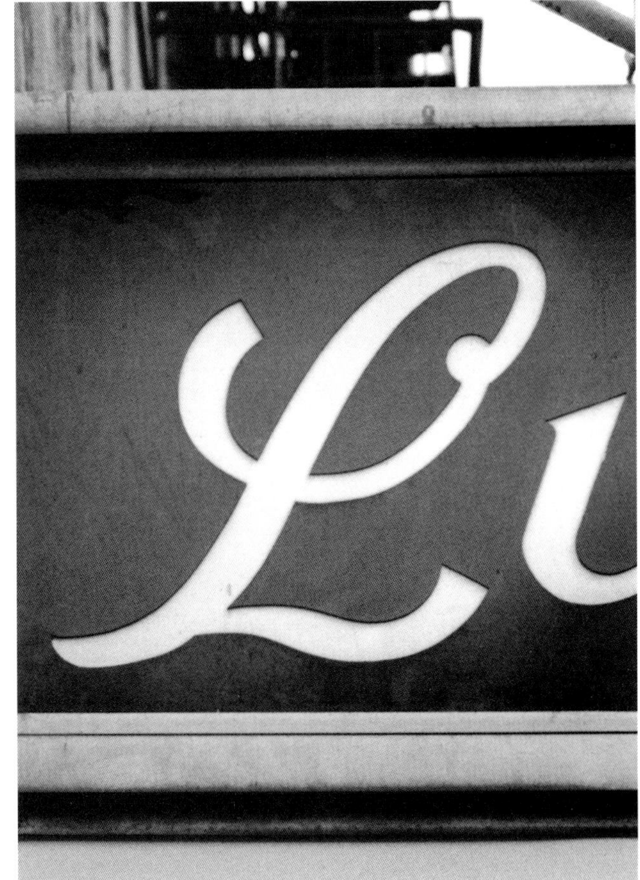
Lu

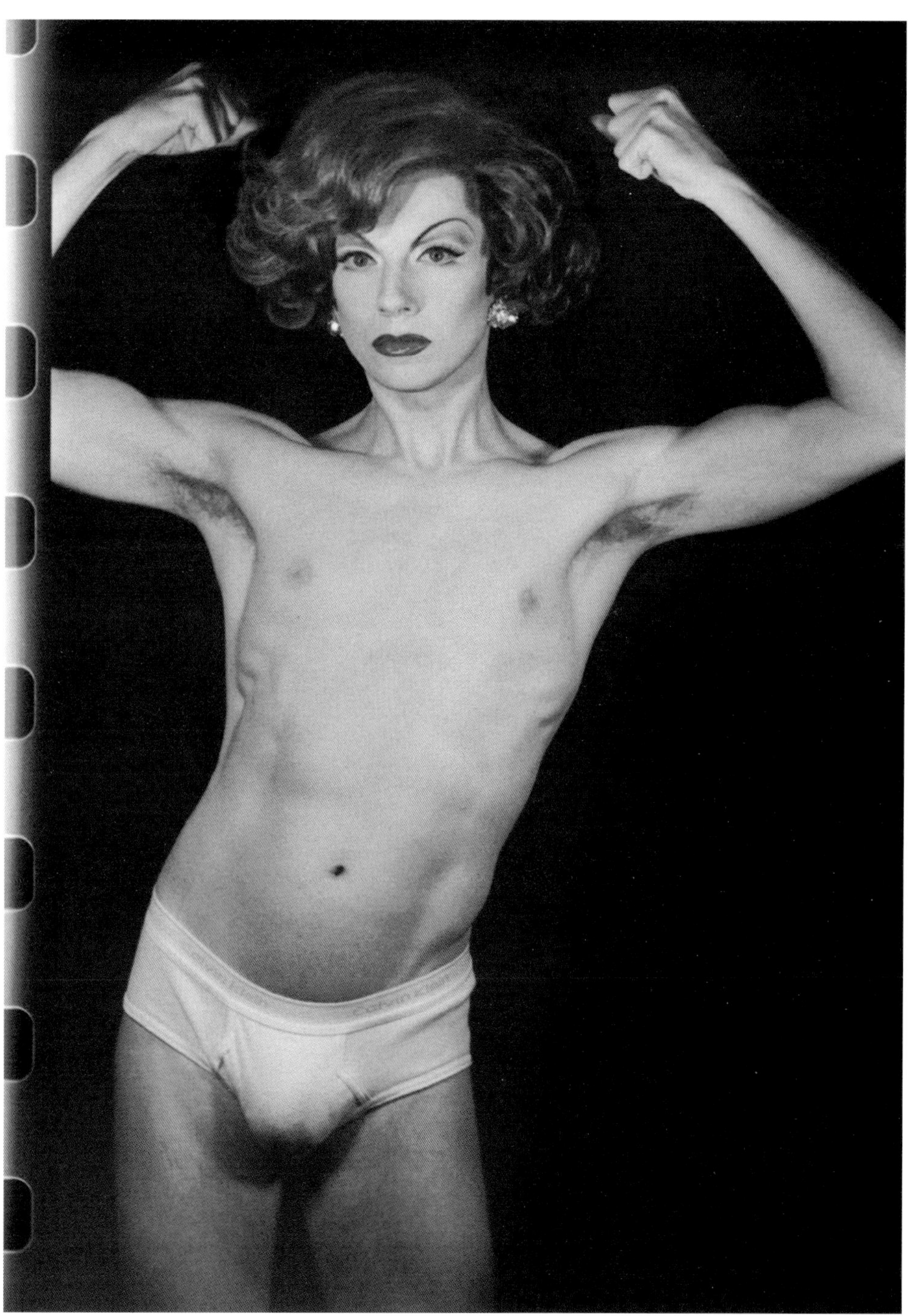

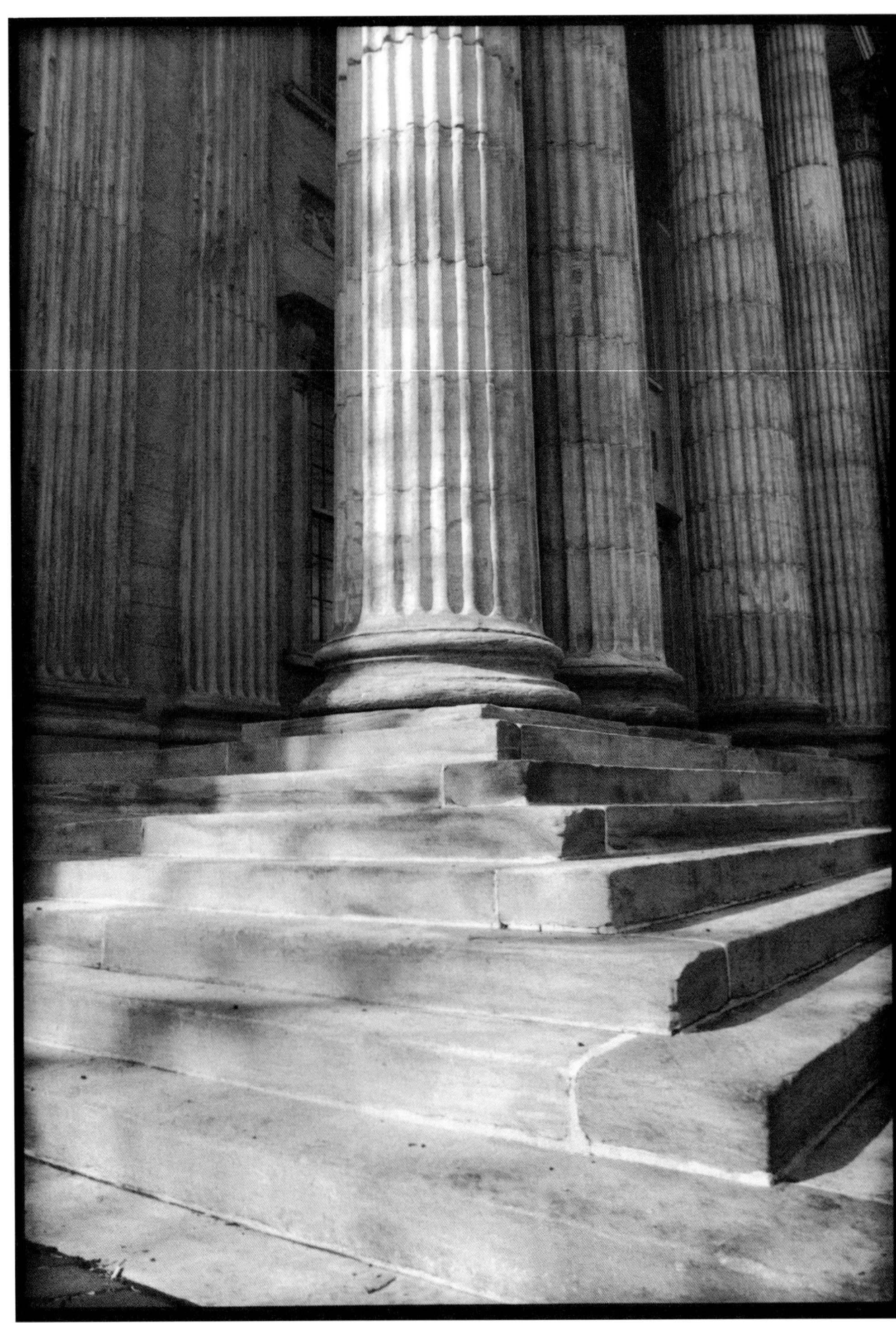

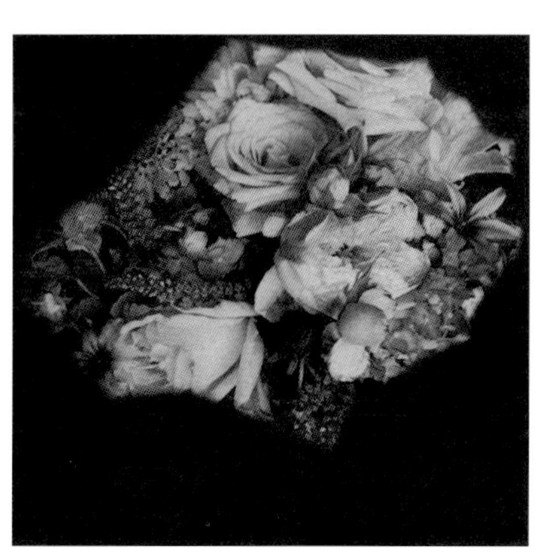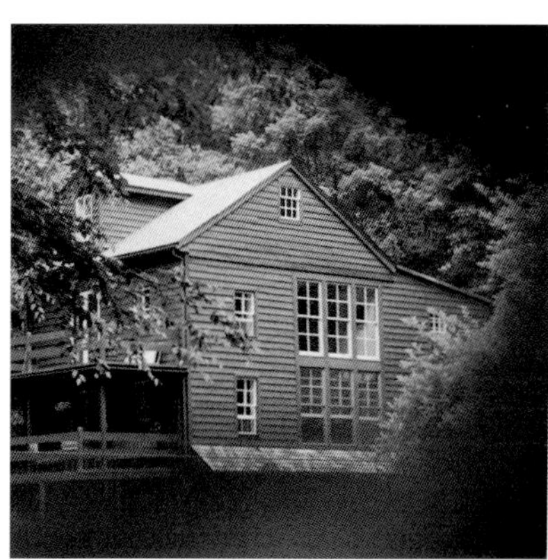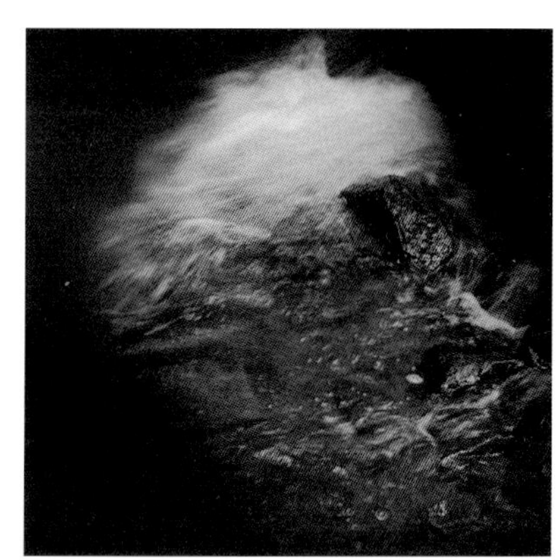

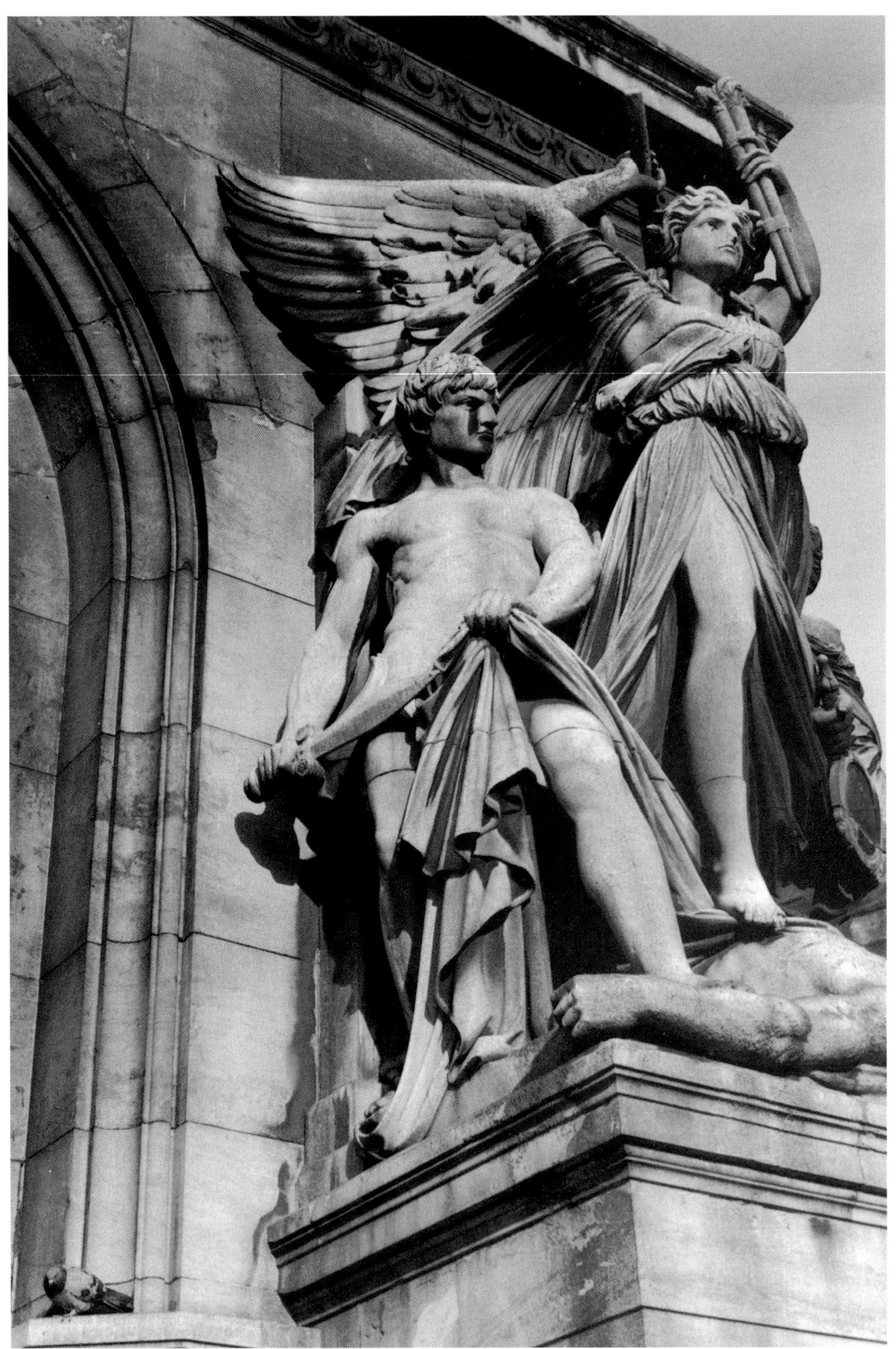

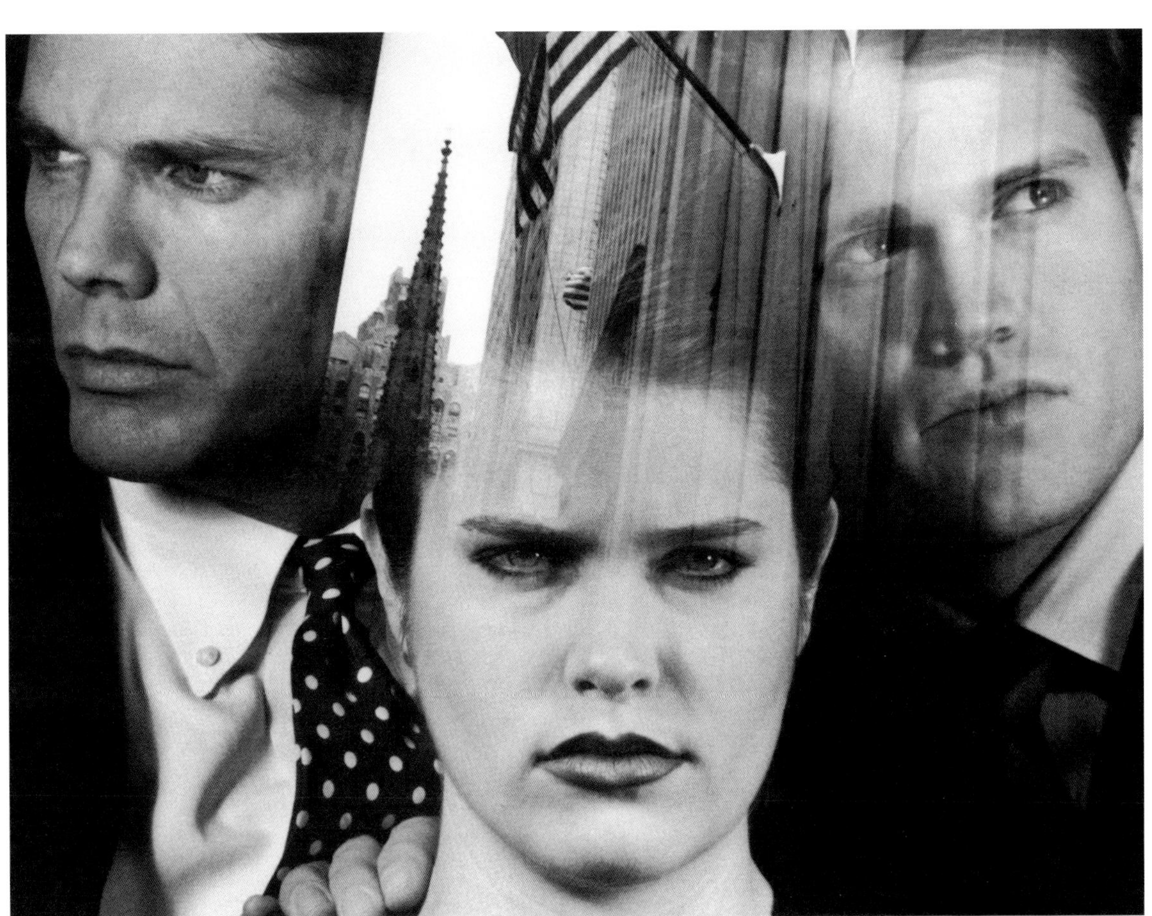

22

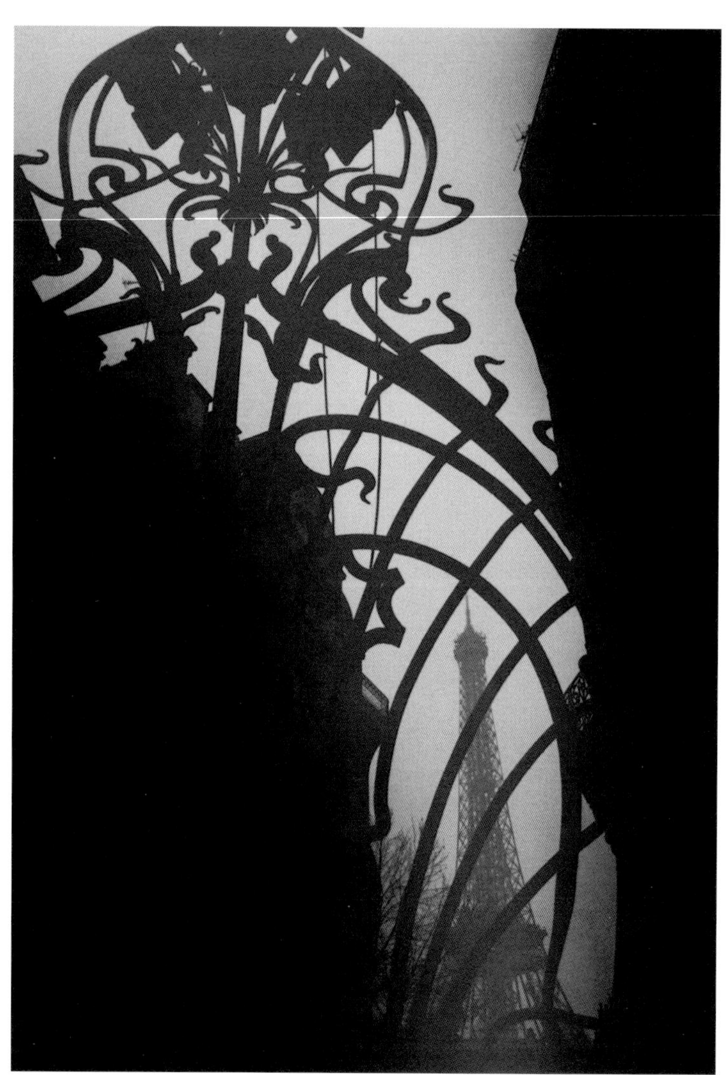

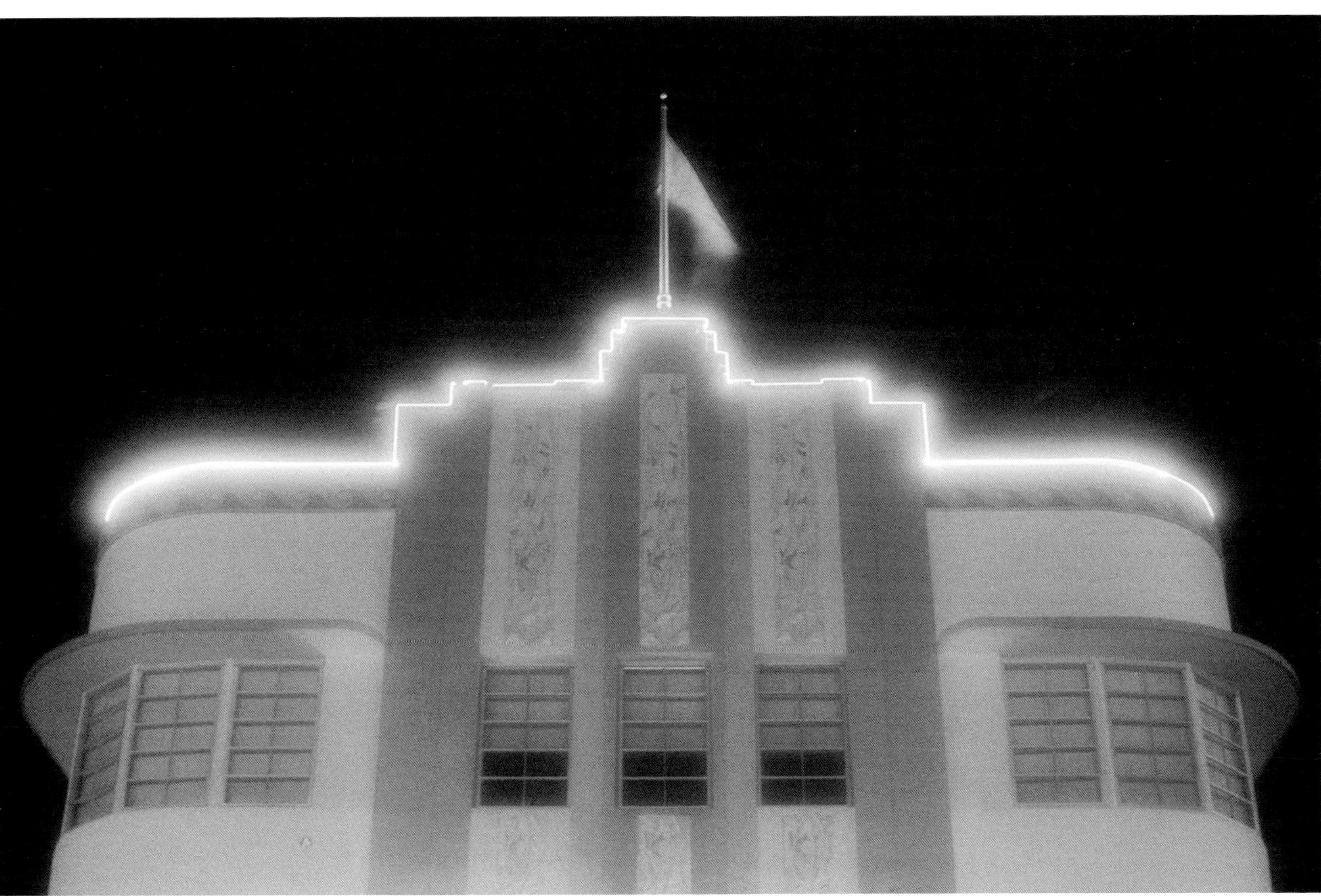

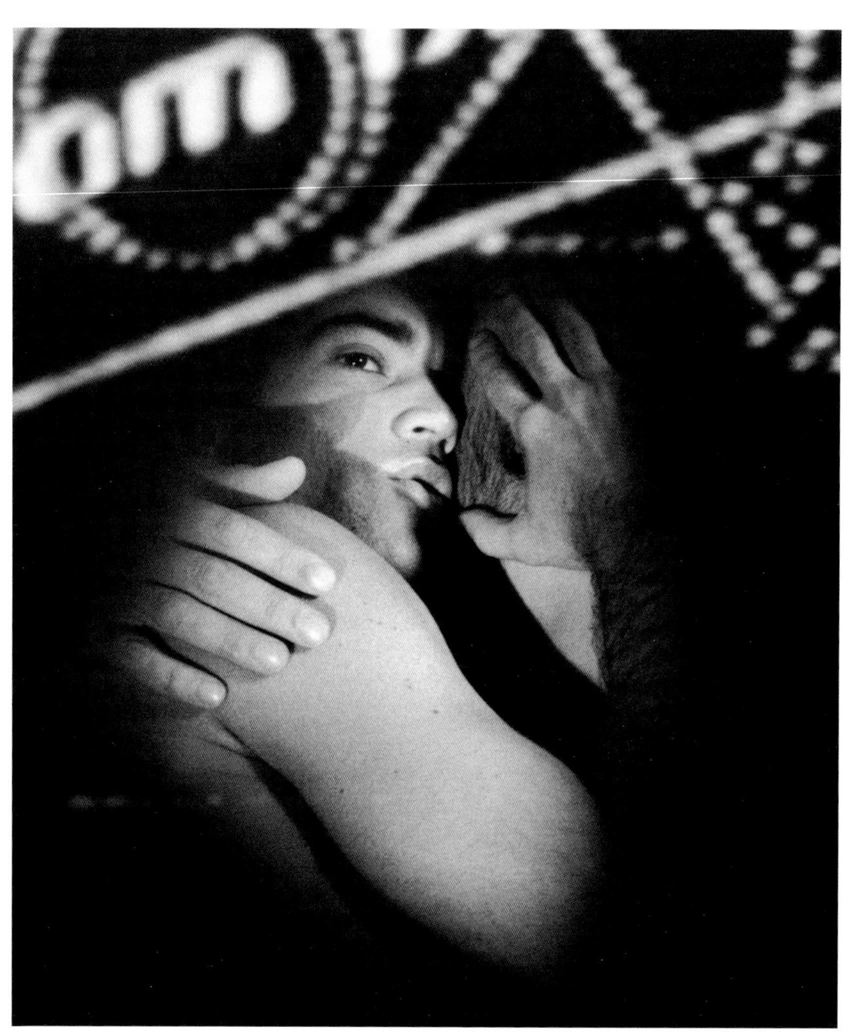

I Went

No restraints. I surrendered completely and I went.
To gratifications that were partly real,
partly careening within my mind —
I went in the glittering night.
And I drank powerful wines, just as
the champions of sensuality drink.

C. P. Cavafy

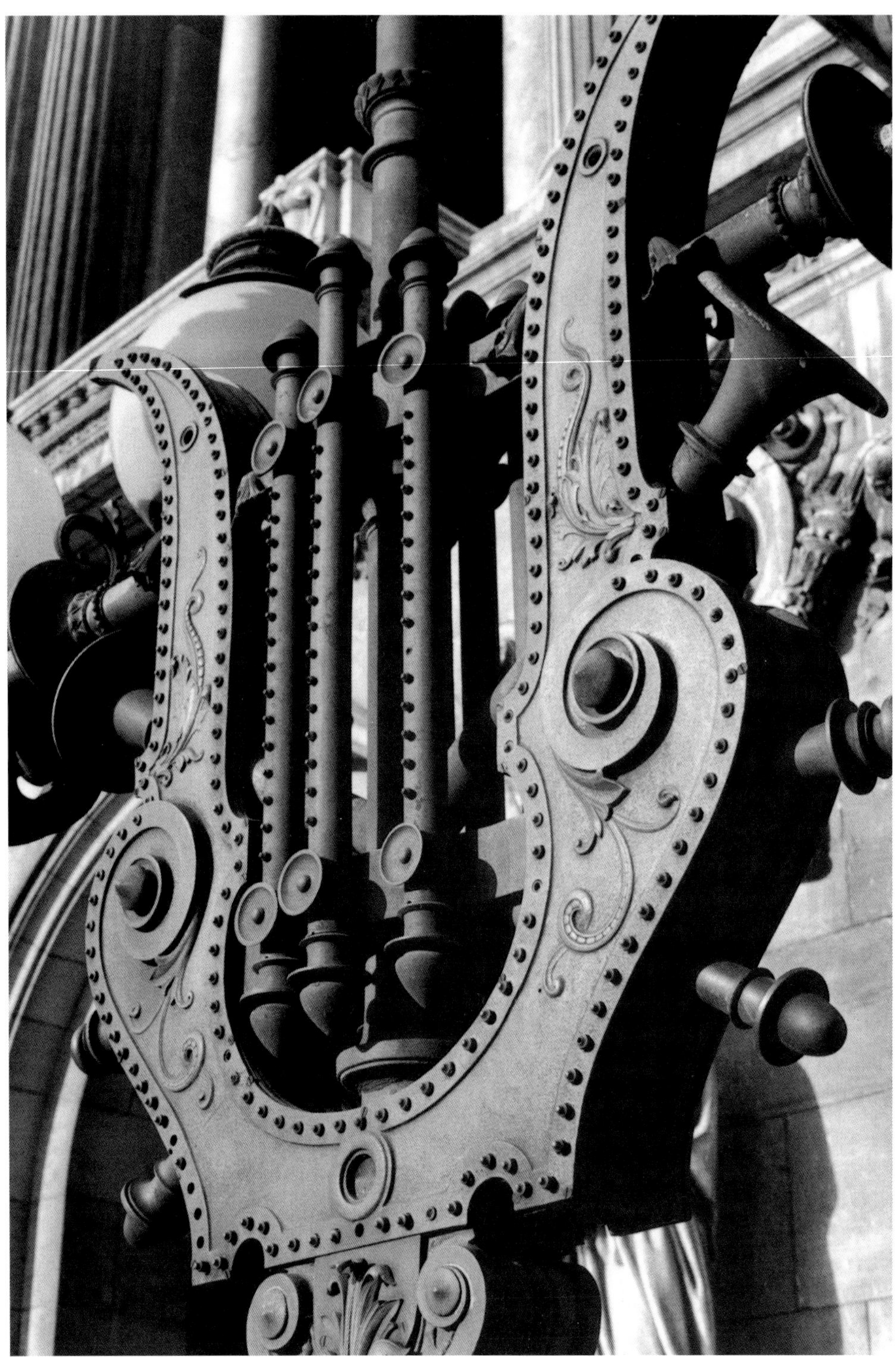

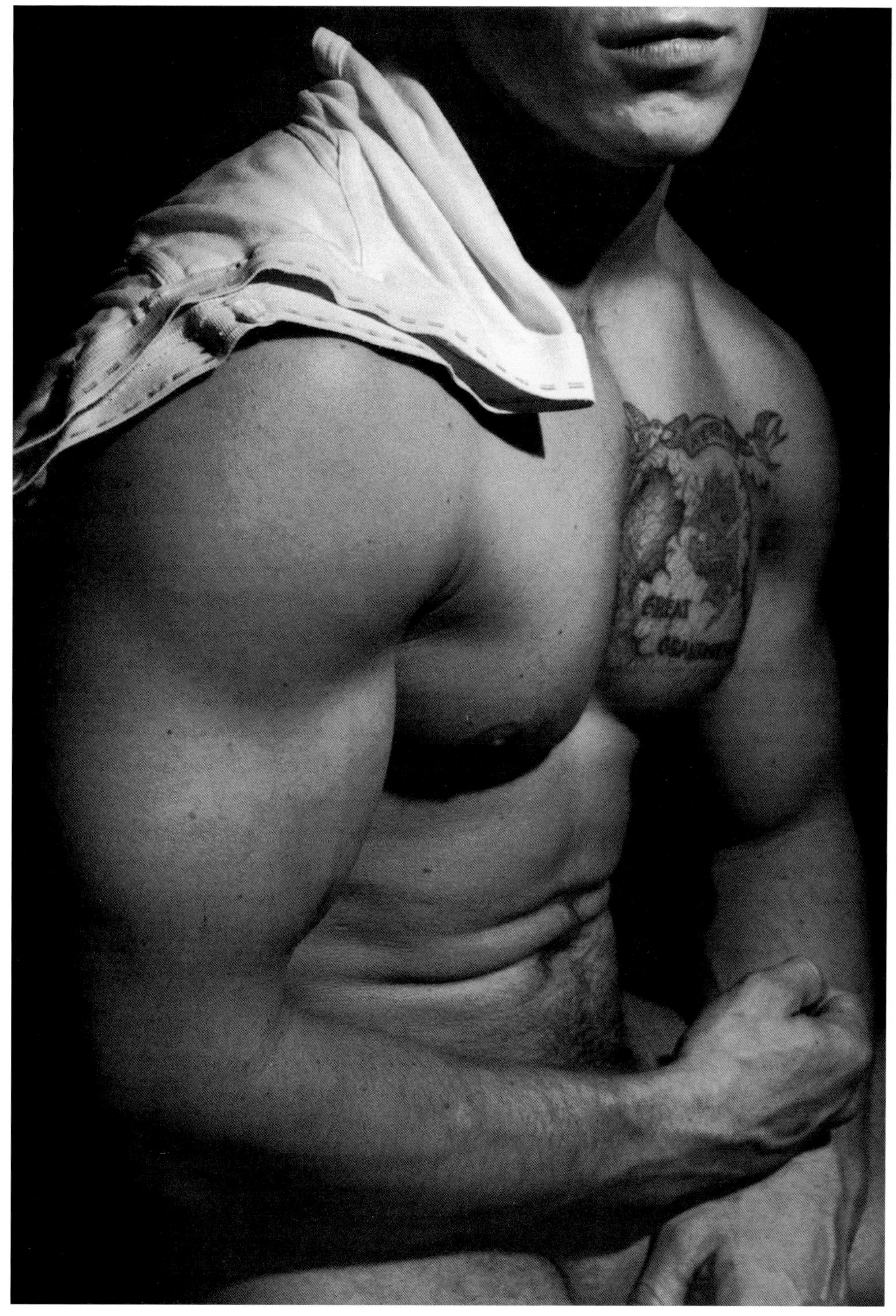

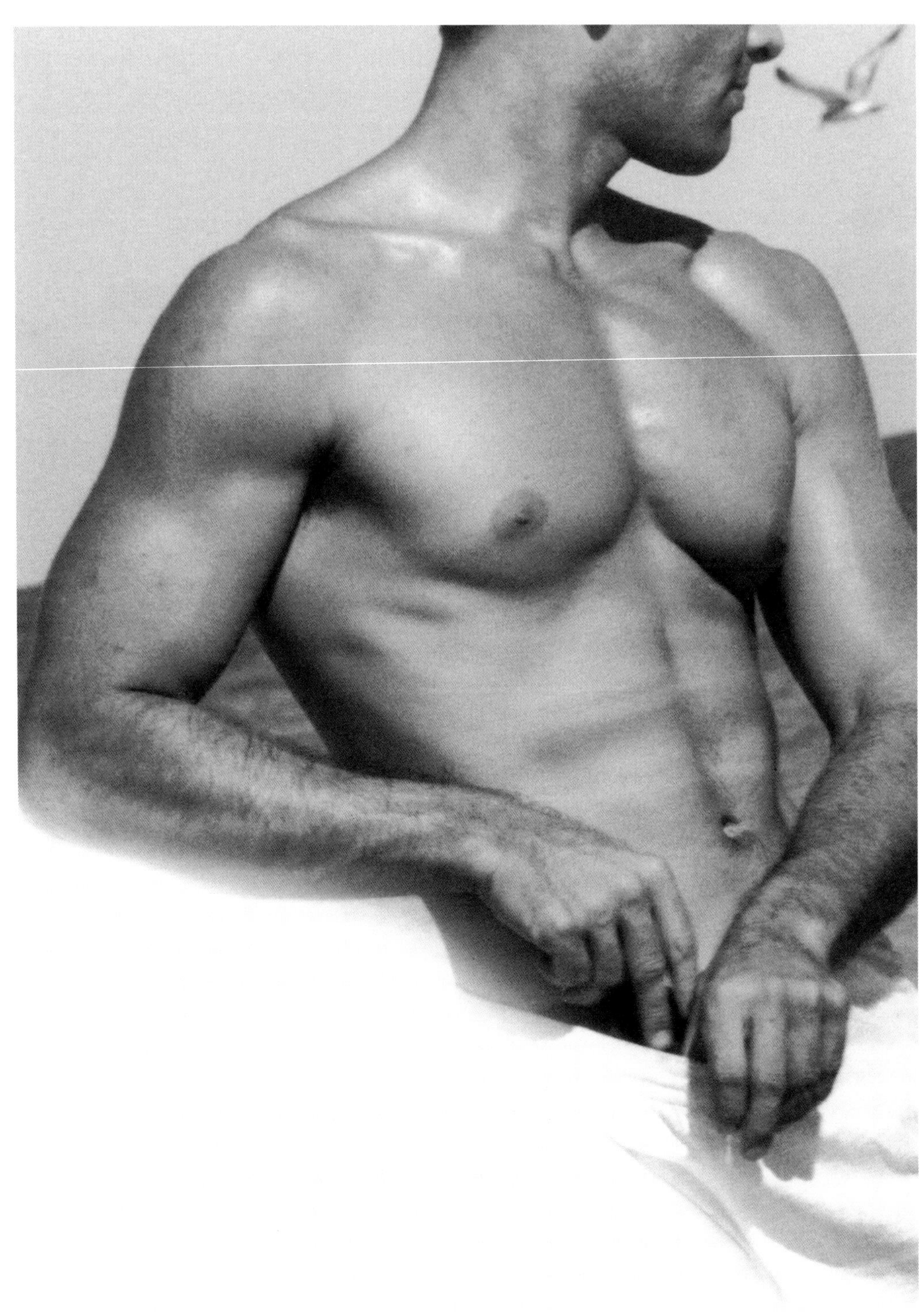

Morning Sea

Here's where I'll stop. Let me too have a look at Nature.
The morning sea and cloudless sky
a brilliant blue, the yellow shore: all
beautiful and magnificently illuminated.

Here's where I'll stop. Let me pretend that this is what I see
(I really saw it for a moment when I first stopped)
instead of seeing, even here, my fantasies,
my recollections, the icons of pleasure.

C. P. Cavafy

Ionic

Because we smashed their statues into pieces,
because we chased them from their shrines —
this hardly means the gods have died.
O land of Ionía, they're still in love with you,
it's you whom their souls still remember.
As an August morning's light breaks over you
Your atmosphere grows effervescent with their living.
And occasionally an airborne adolescent shape
indeterminate, stepping swiftly,
speeds its way above your crested hills.

C. P. Cavafy

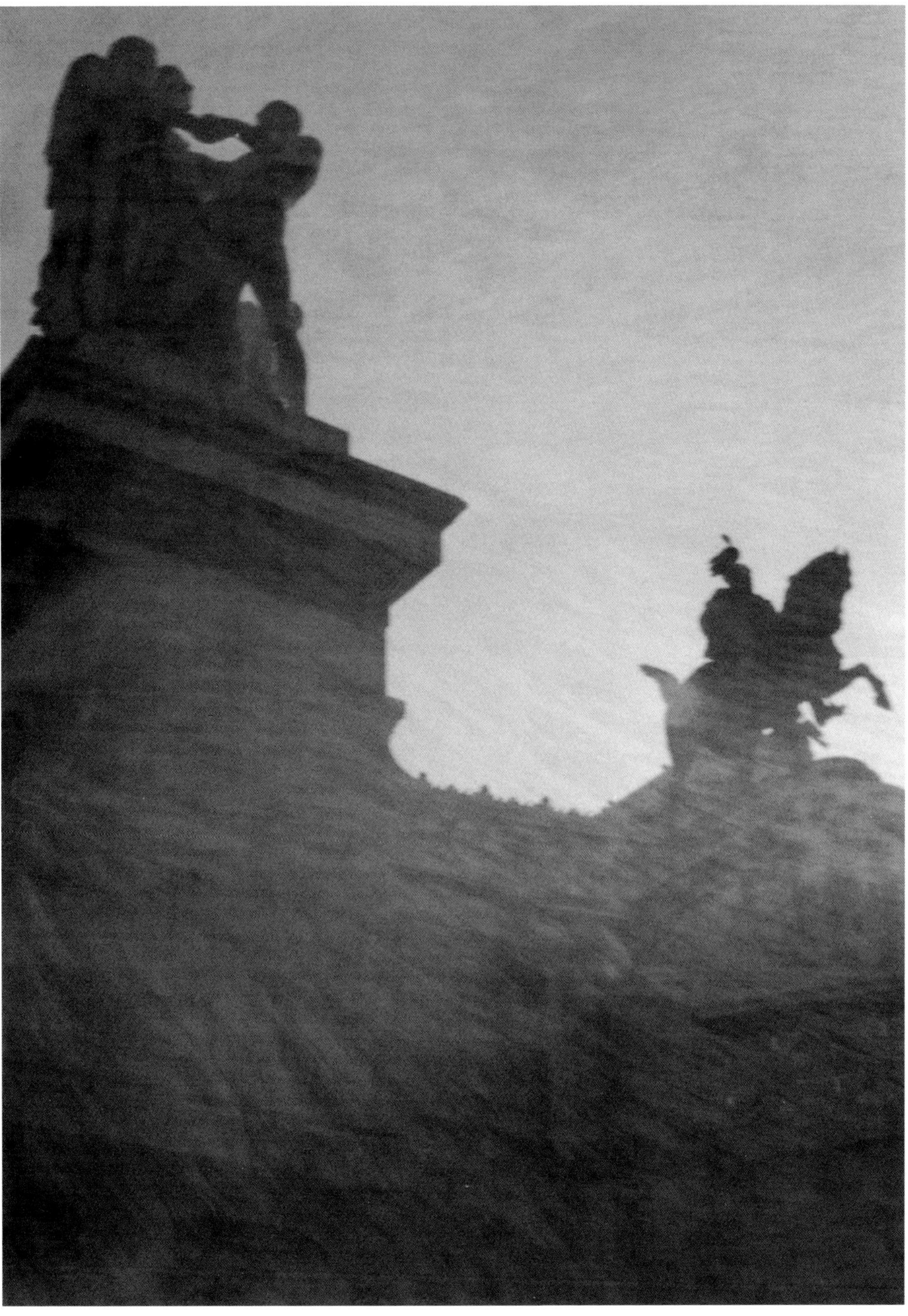

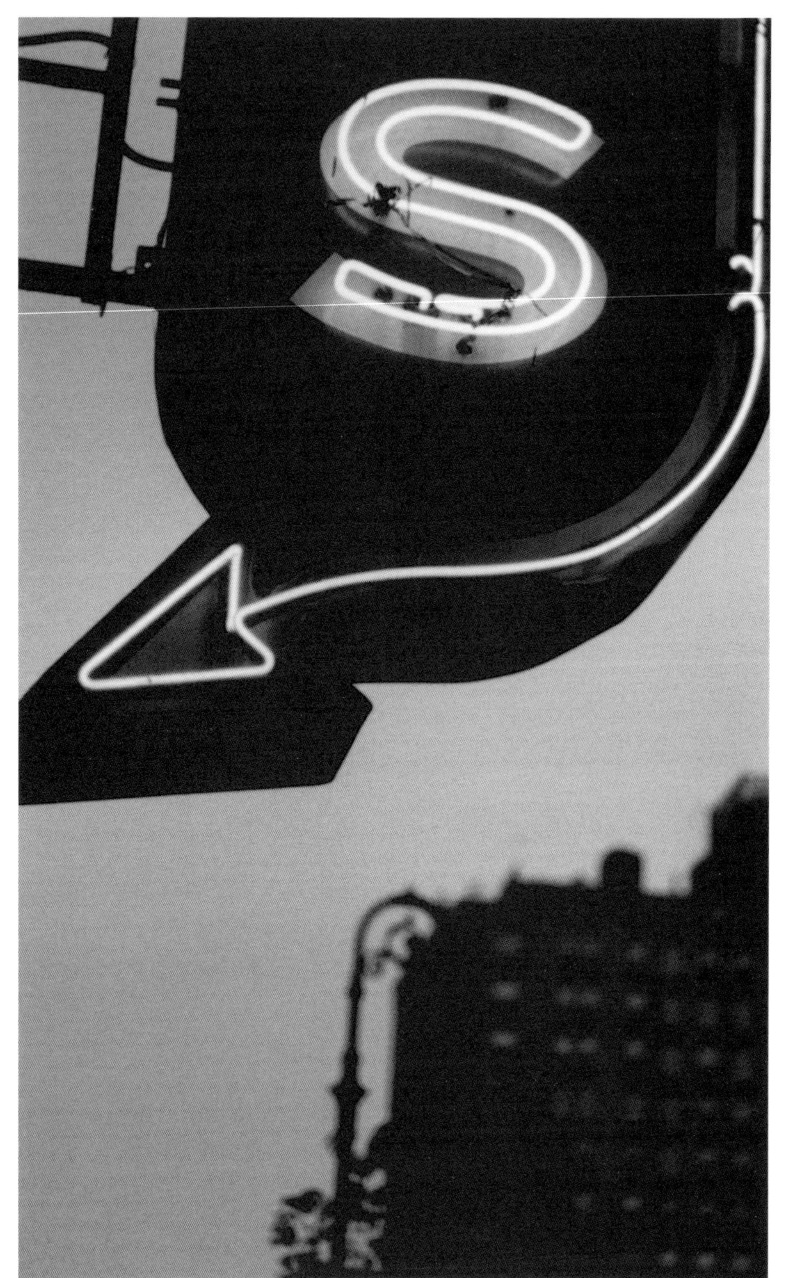

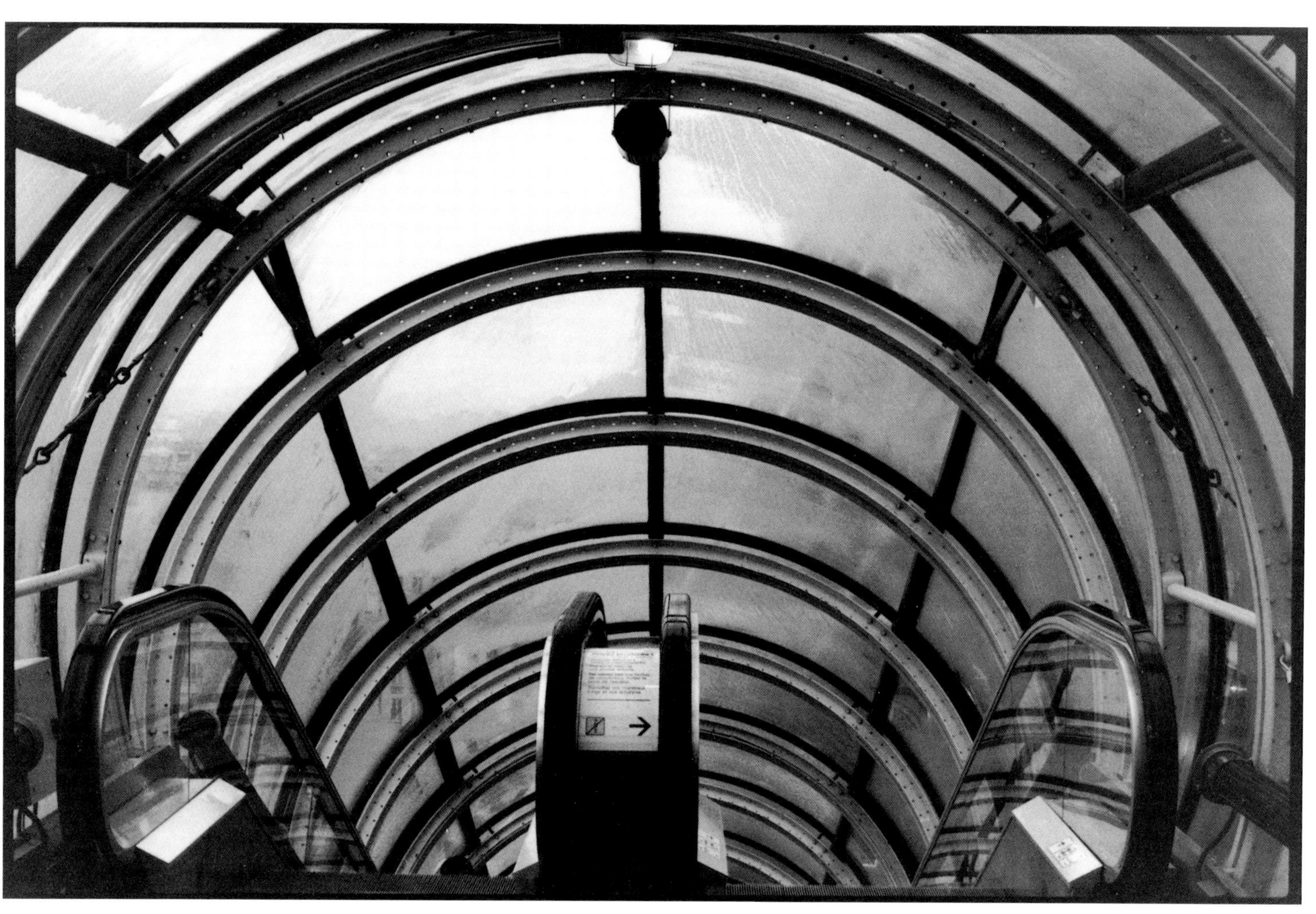

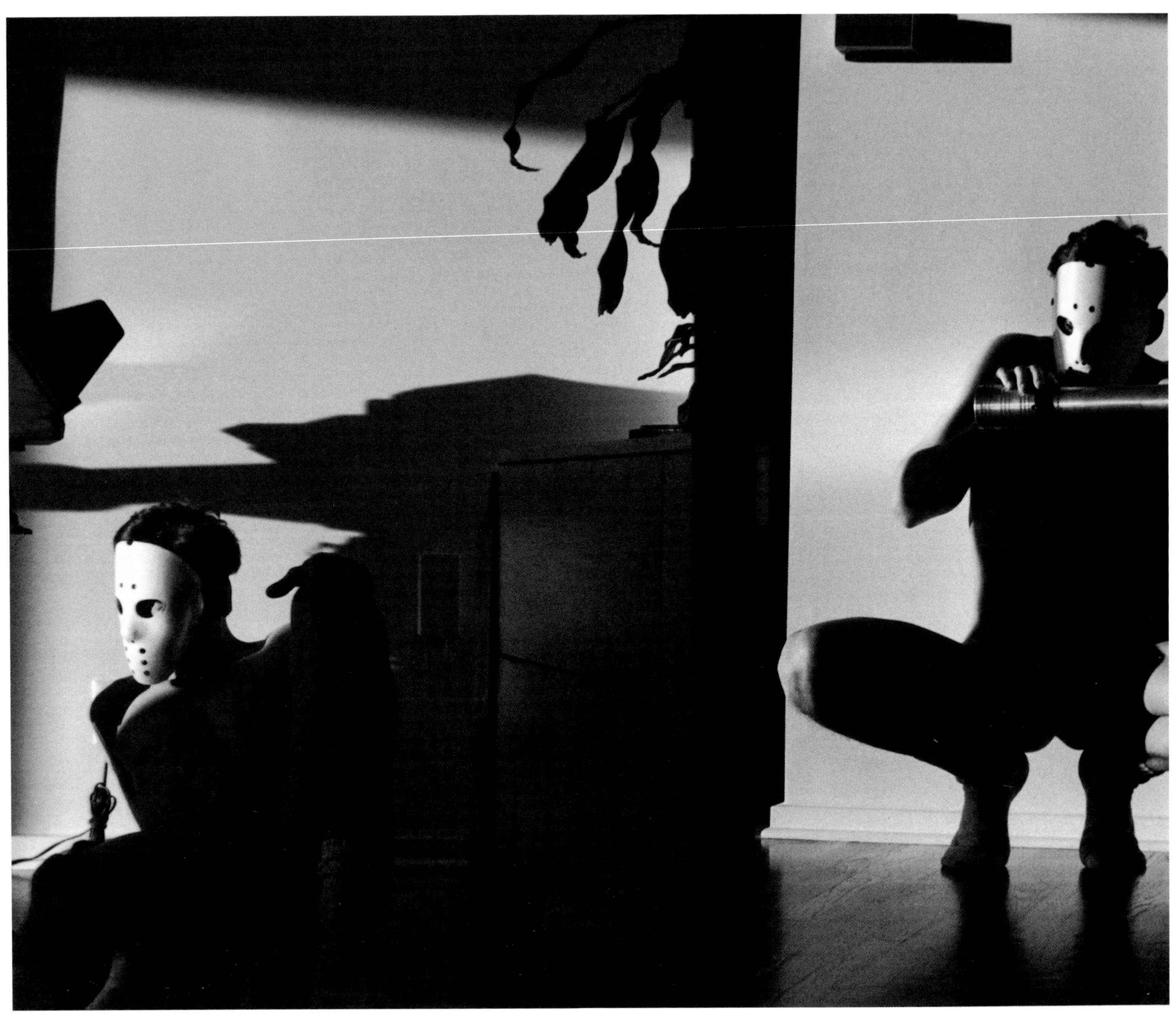

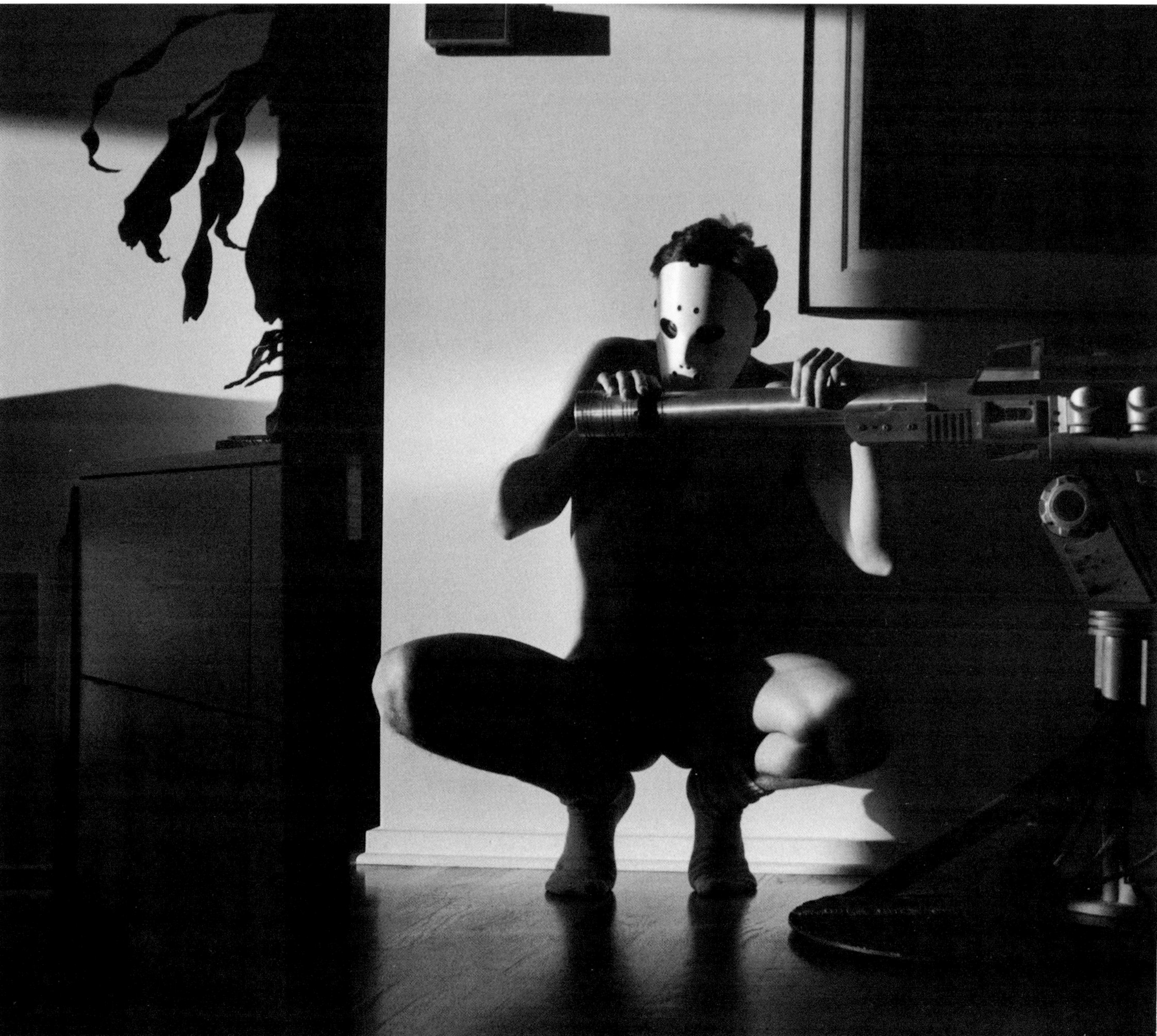

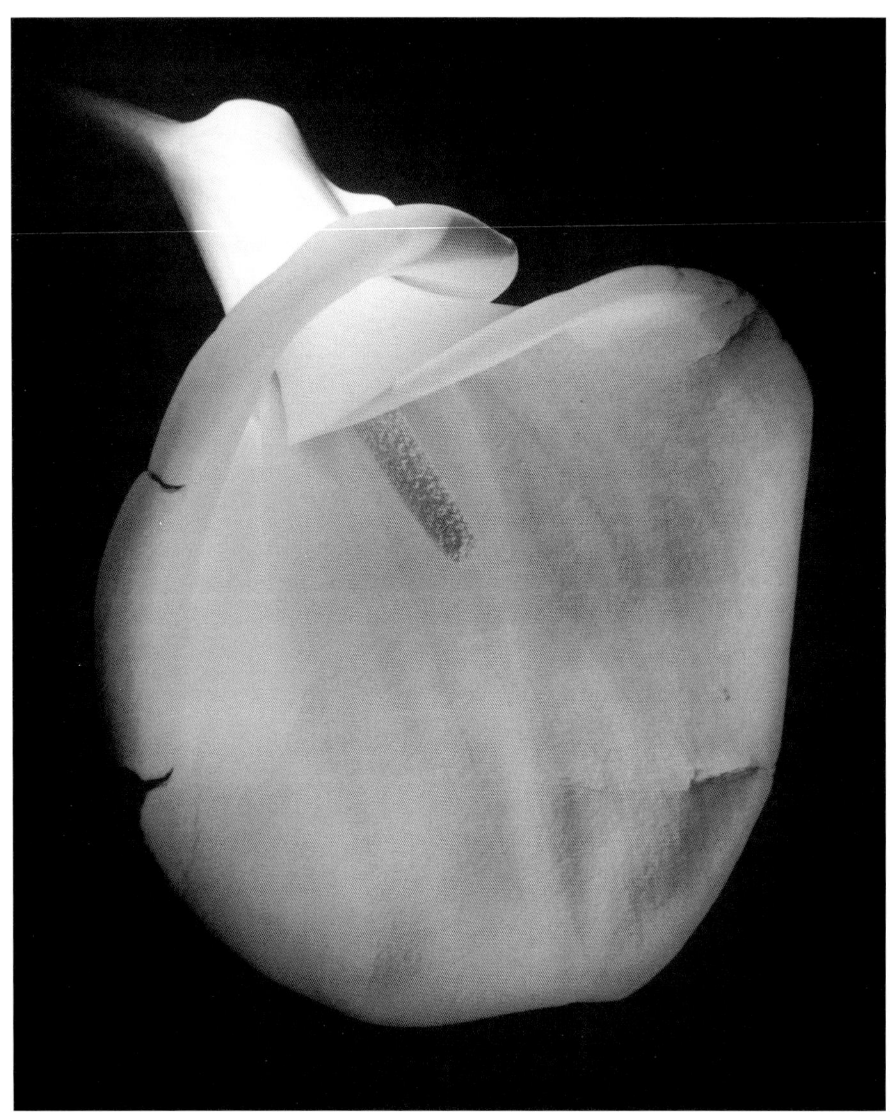

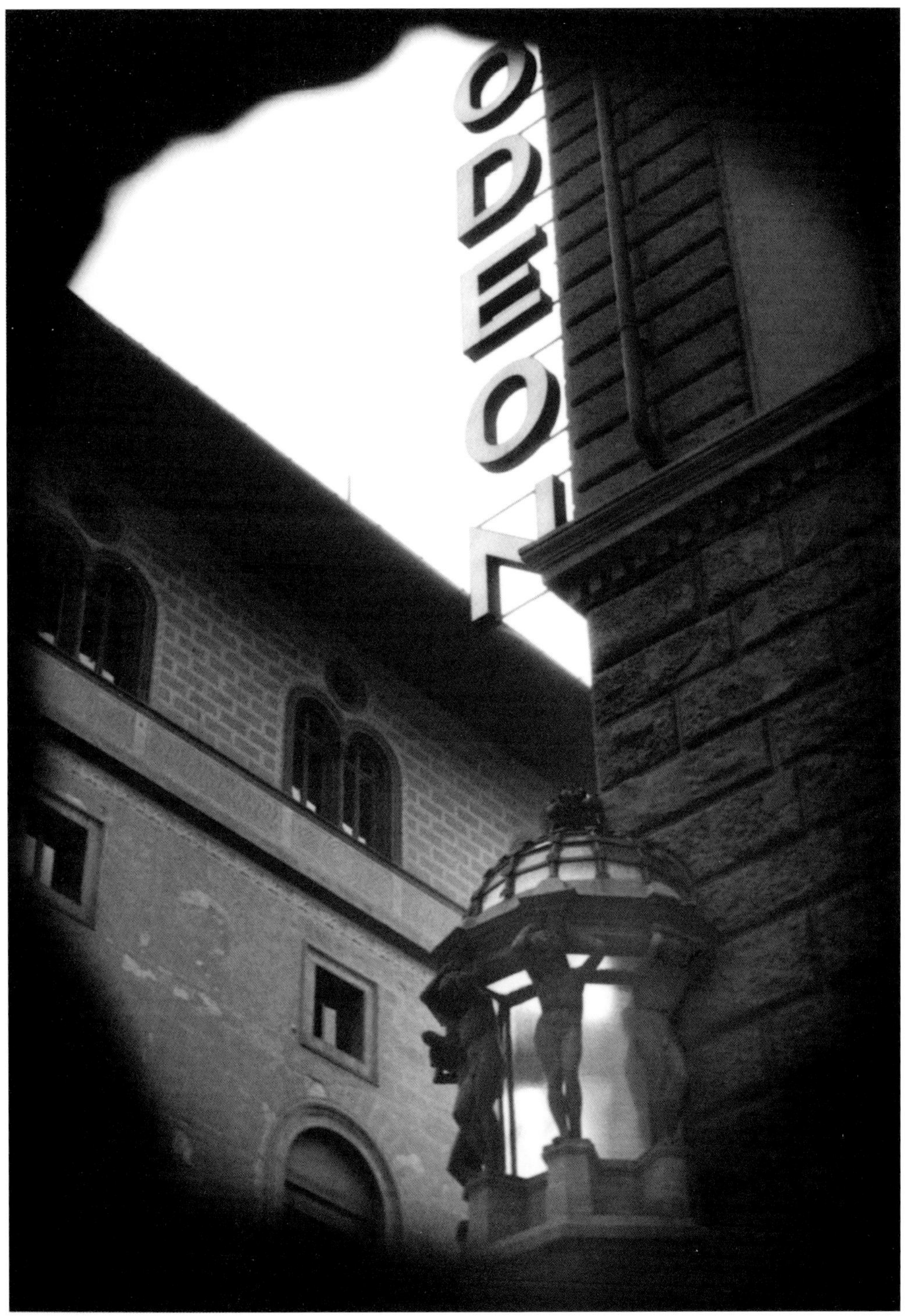

ODEON
FI

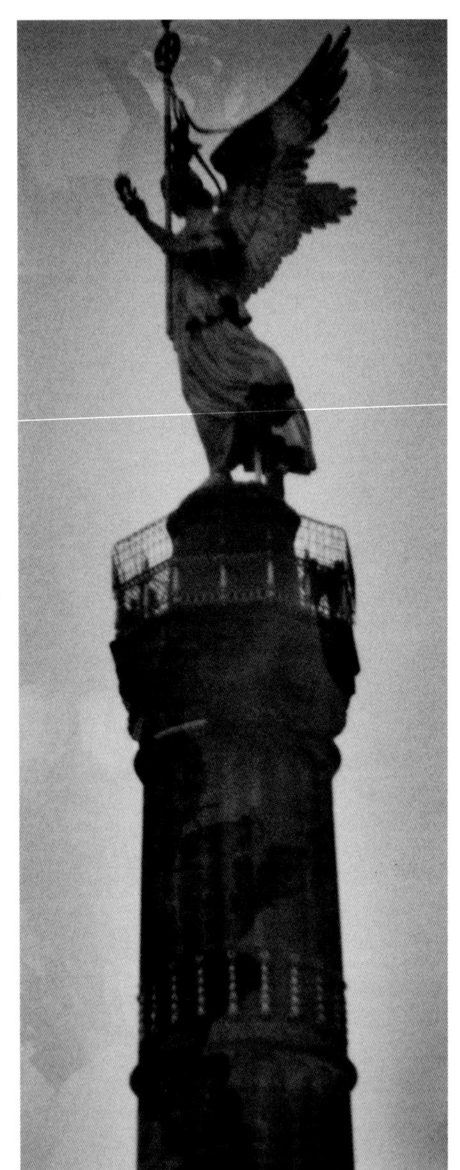

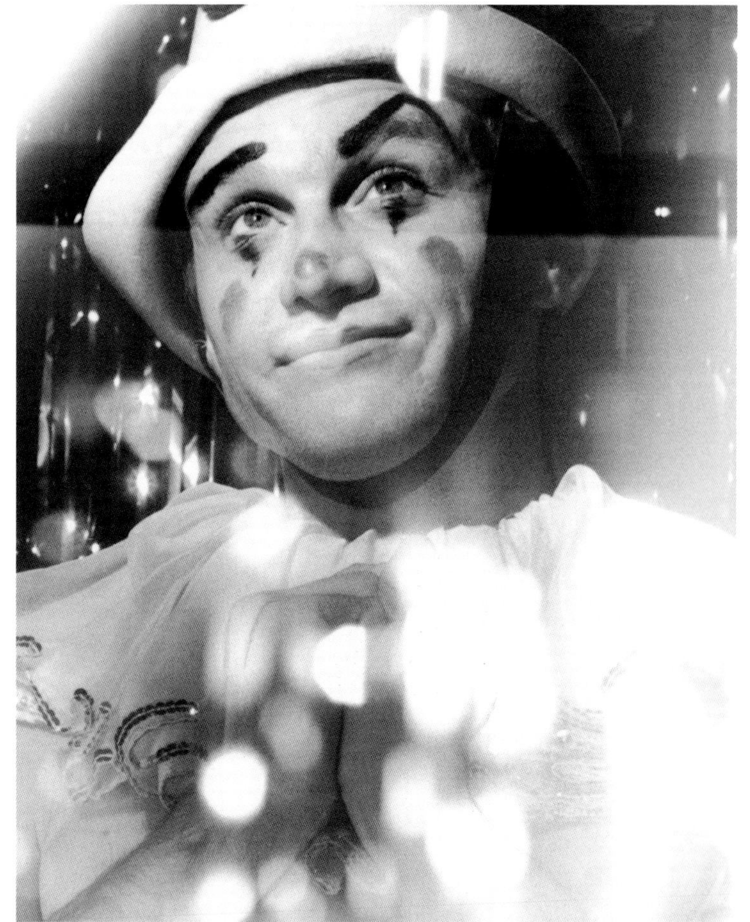

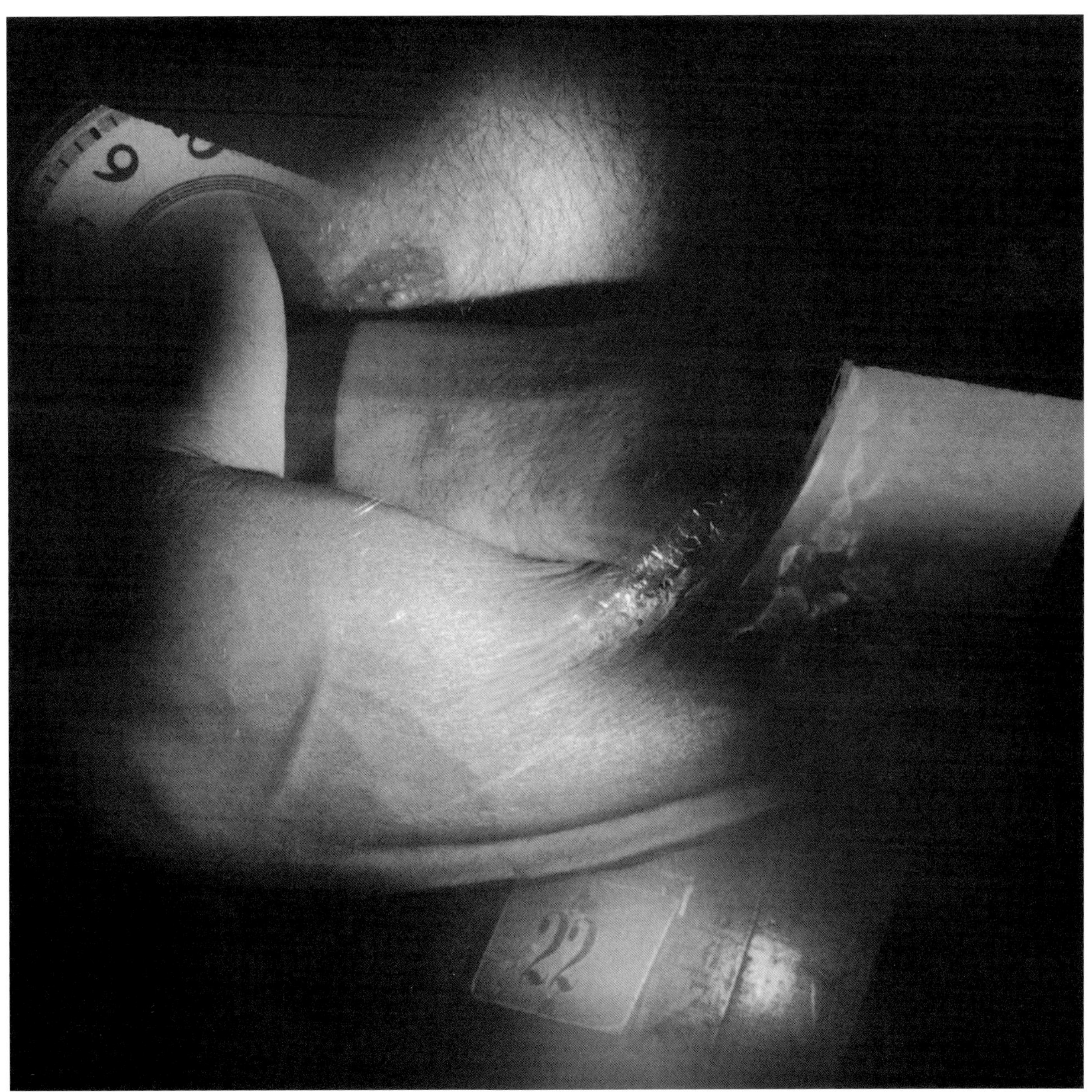

Tomb of Iasís

Here I lie: Iasís. Of all who lived in this great city, I was renowned
for being the most beautiful boy.
Admired by men of deep learning — and also by the less profound,
the common folk. Both these tributes gave equal joy

to me. But being taken so often for a Narcissus, for some young Hermes
wore me out: I indulged myself to death. Passerby,
if you're Alexandrian you won't judge me harshly. You know how feverishly they burn, these
impulses that drive our kind. Of all pleasures, we live for those most high.

C. P. Cavafy

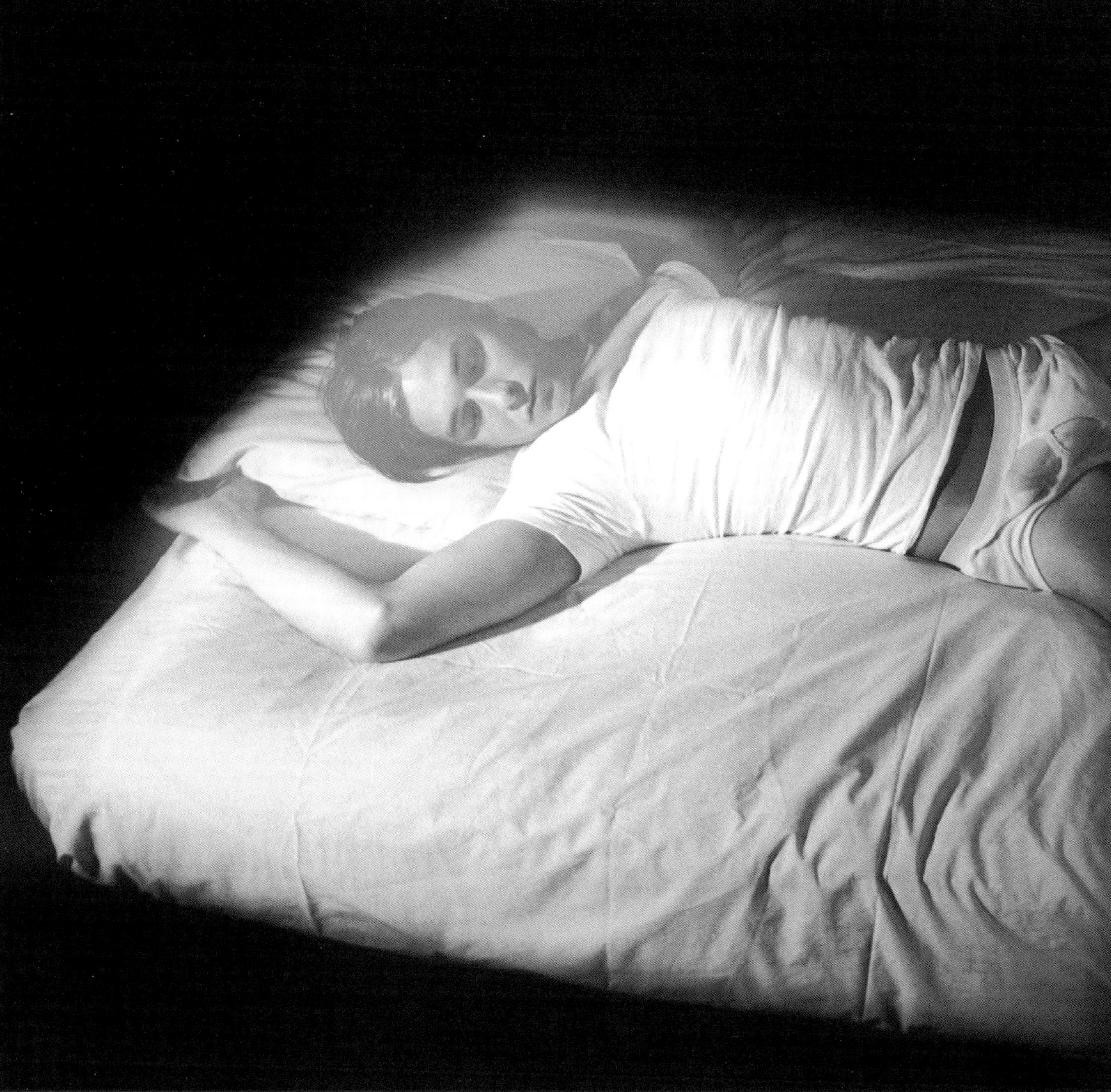

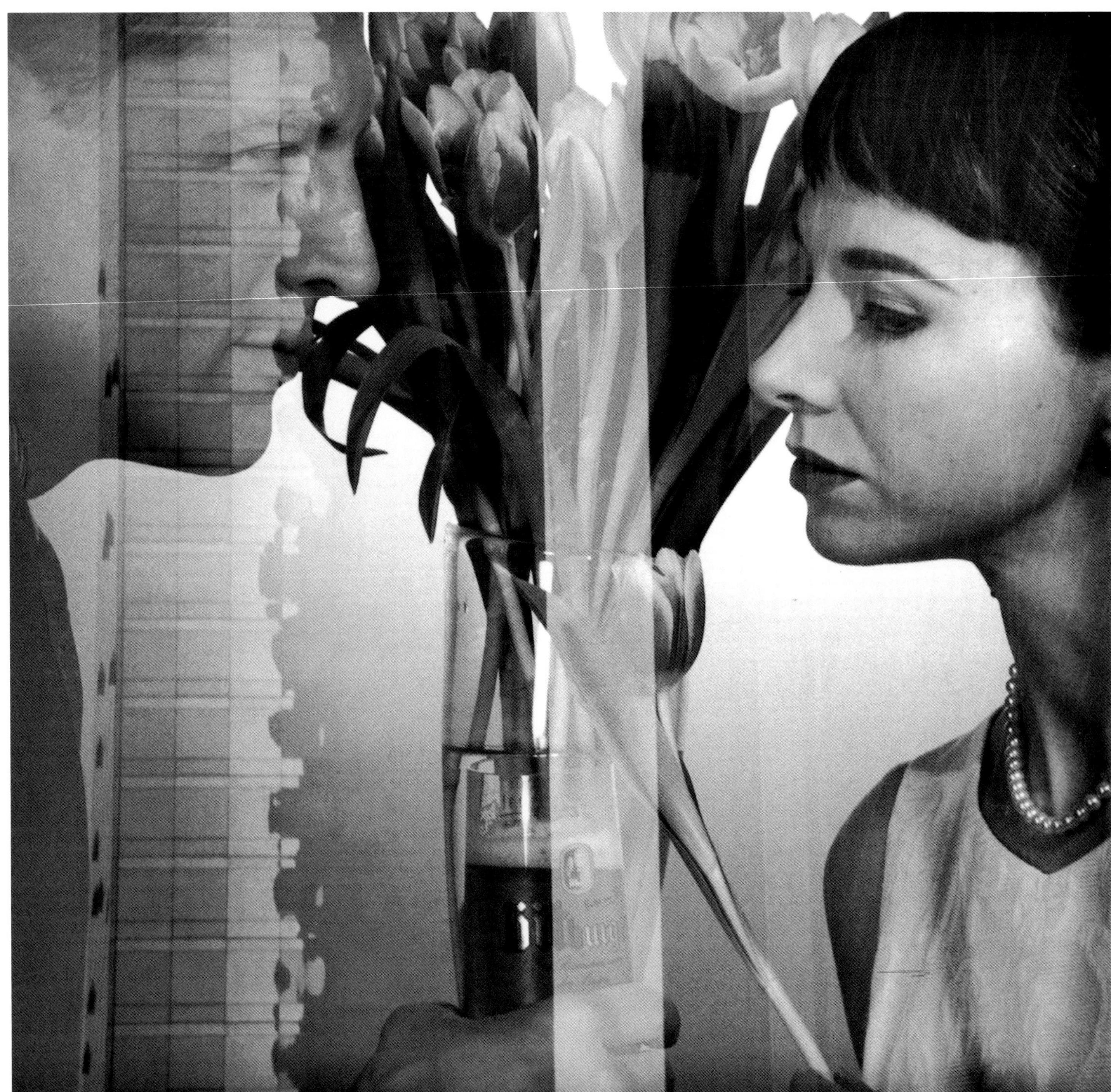

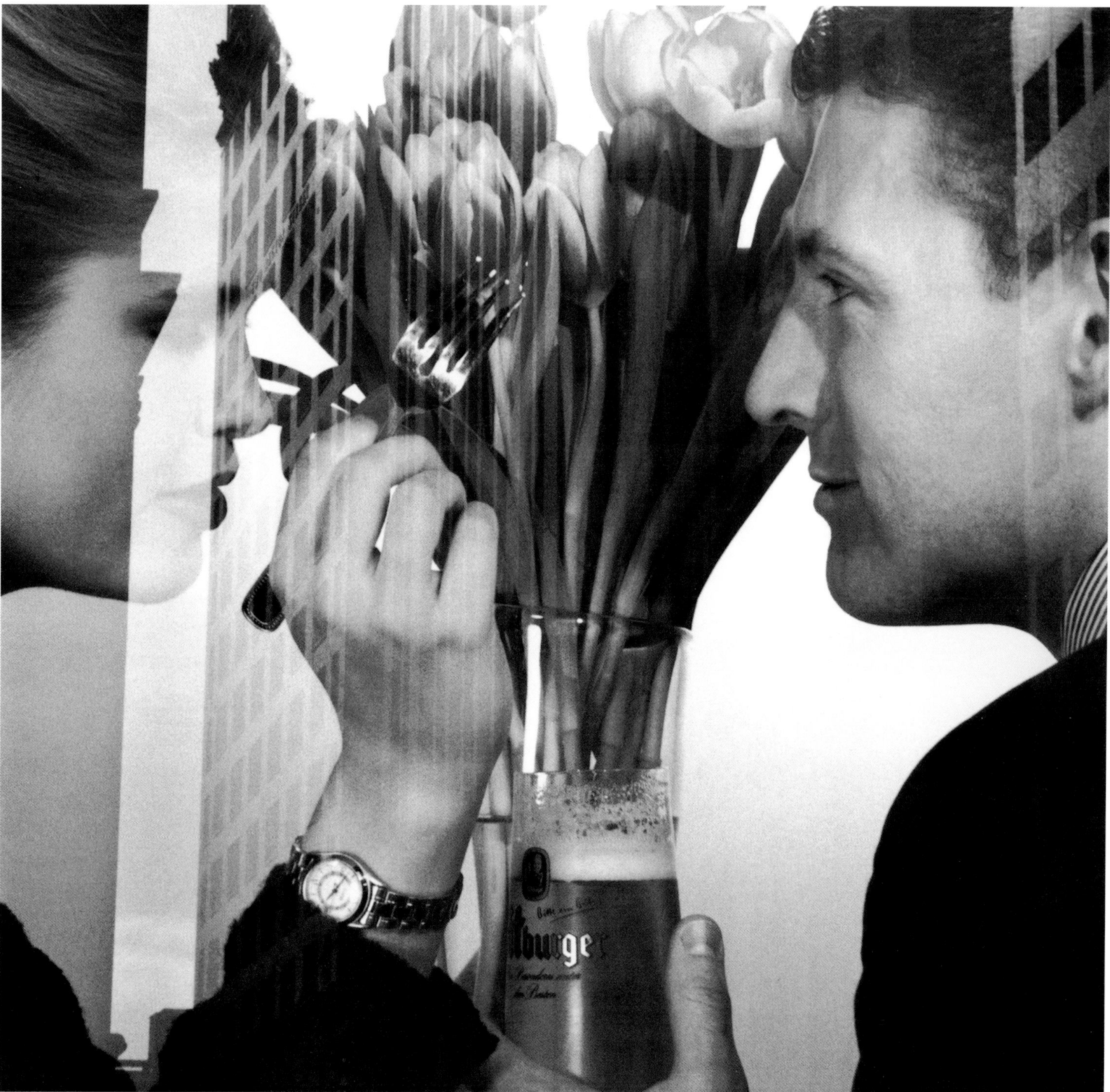

Bitte ein Bit
lburger

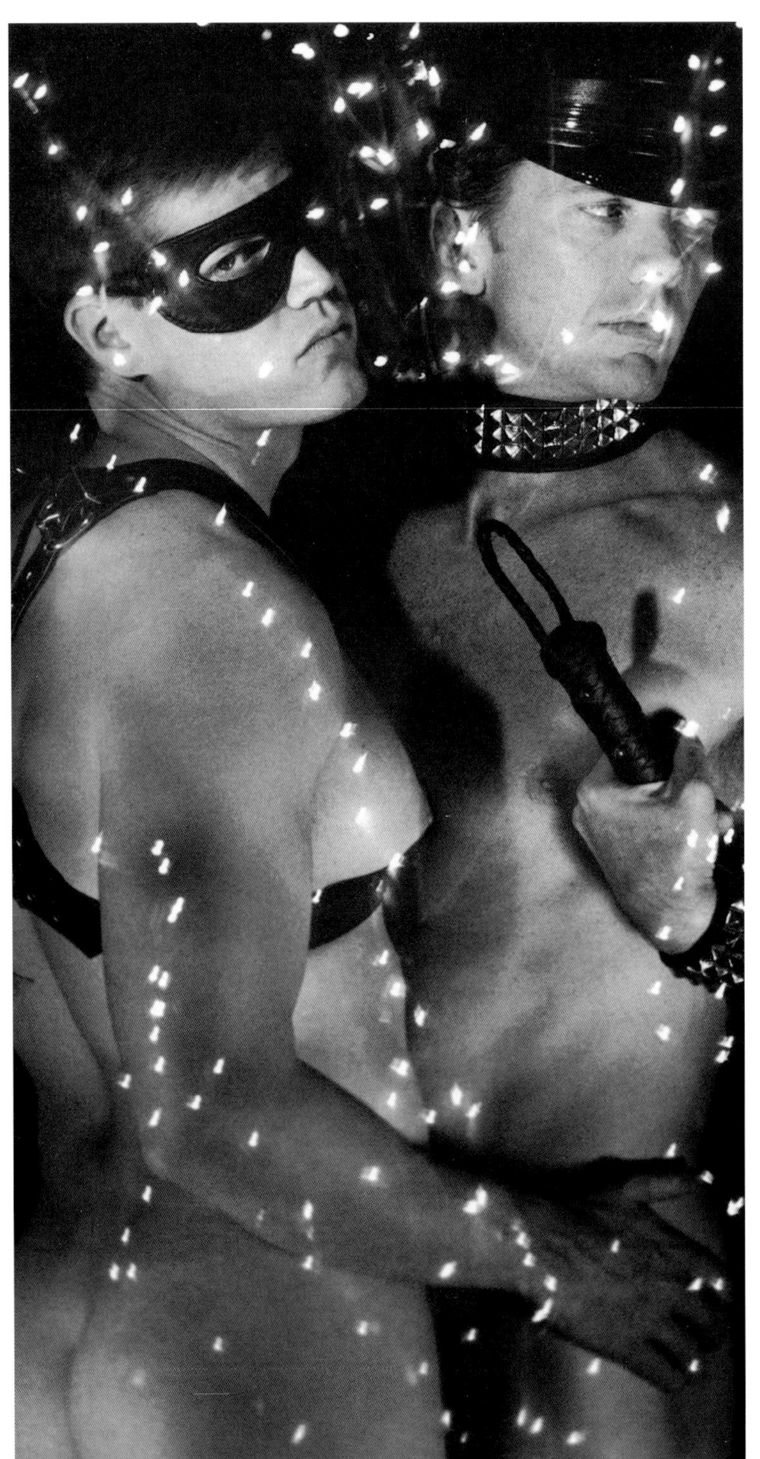

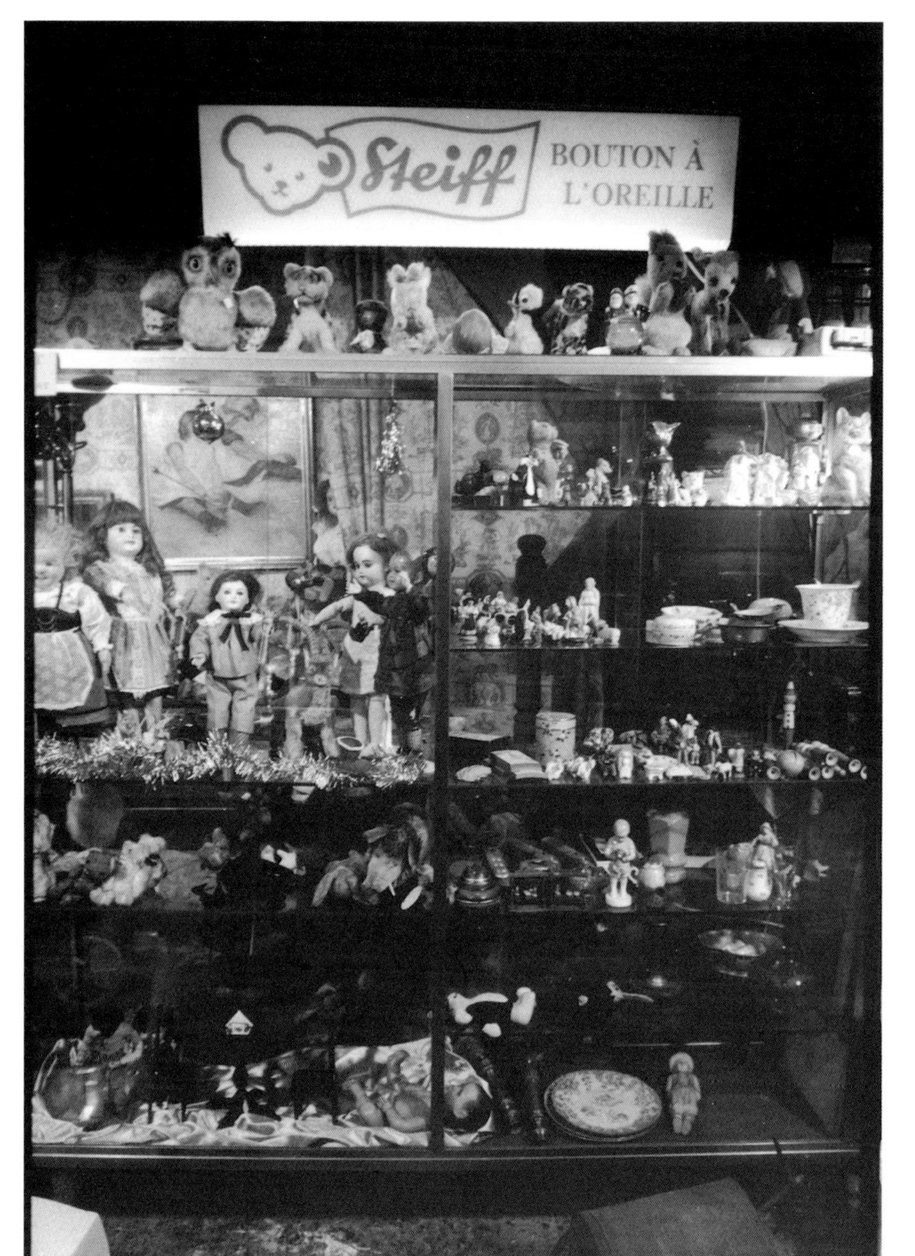
Steiff
BOUTON À
L'OREILLE

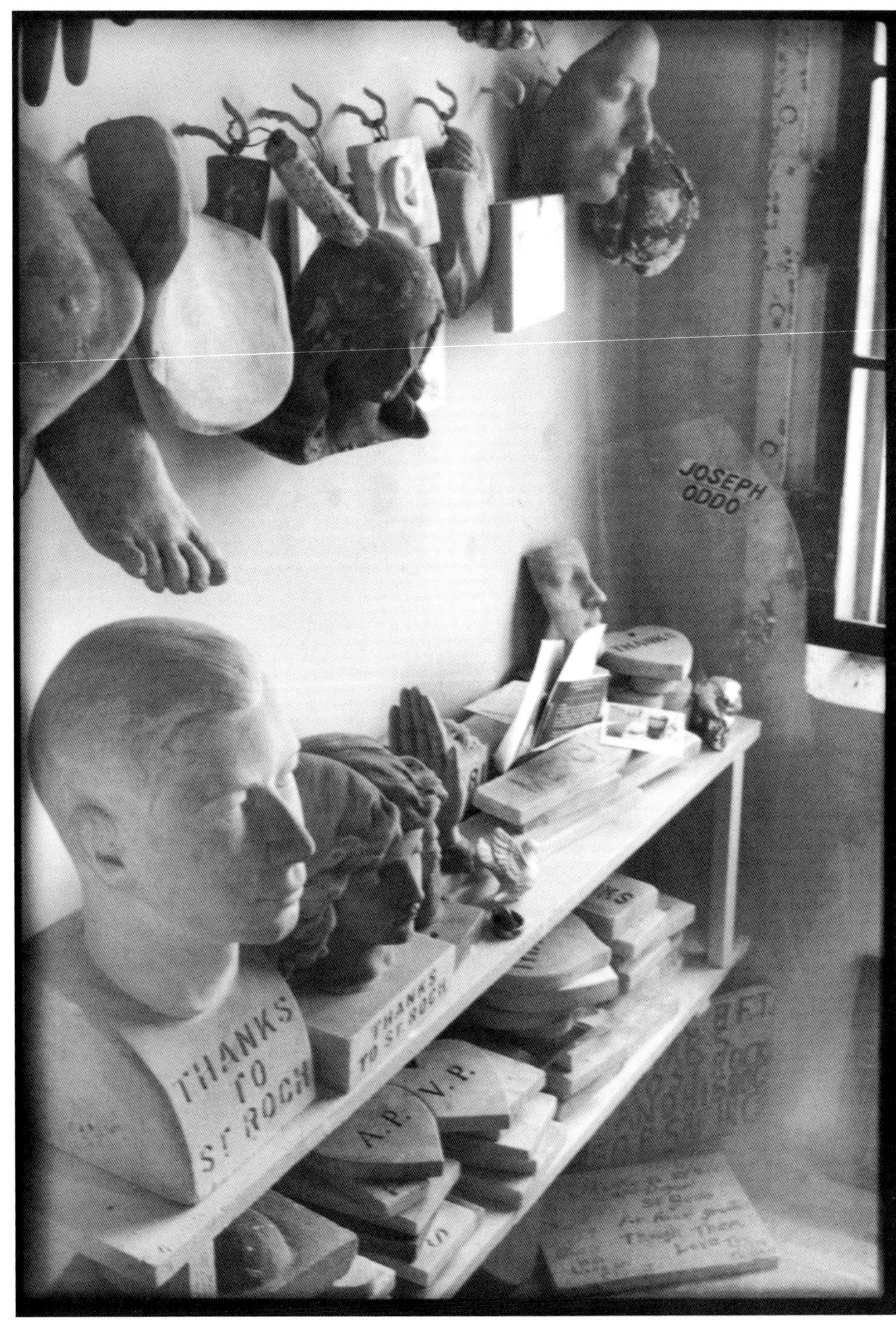
JOSEPH
ODDO
THANKS
TO
St ROCH
THANKS
TO St ROCH
A.P.N.P.

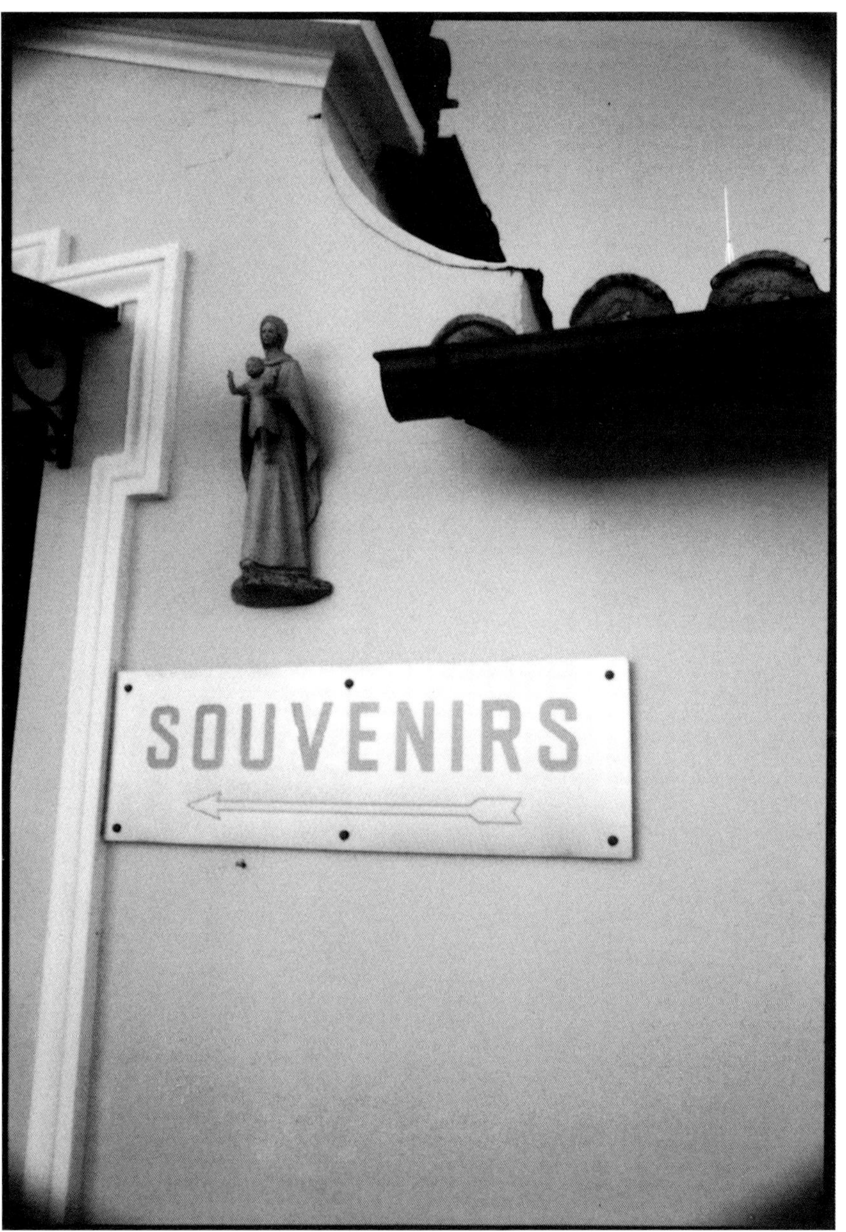
SOUVENIRS

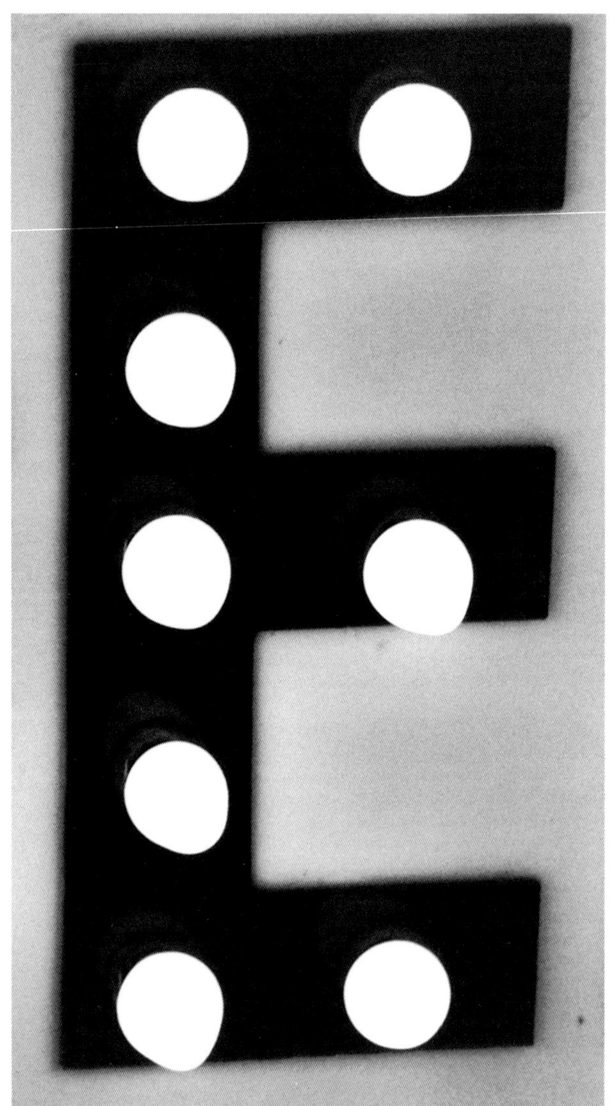

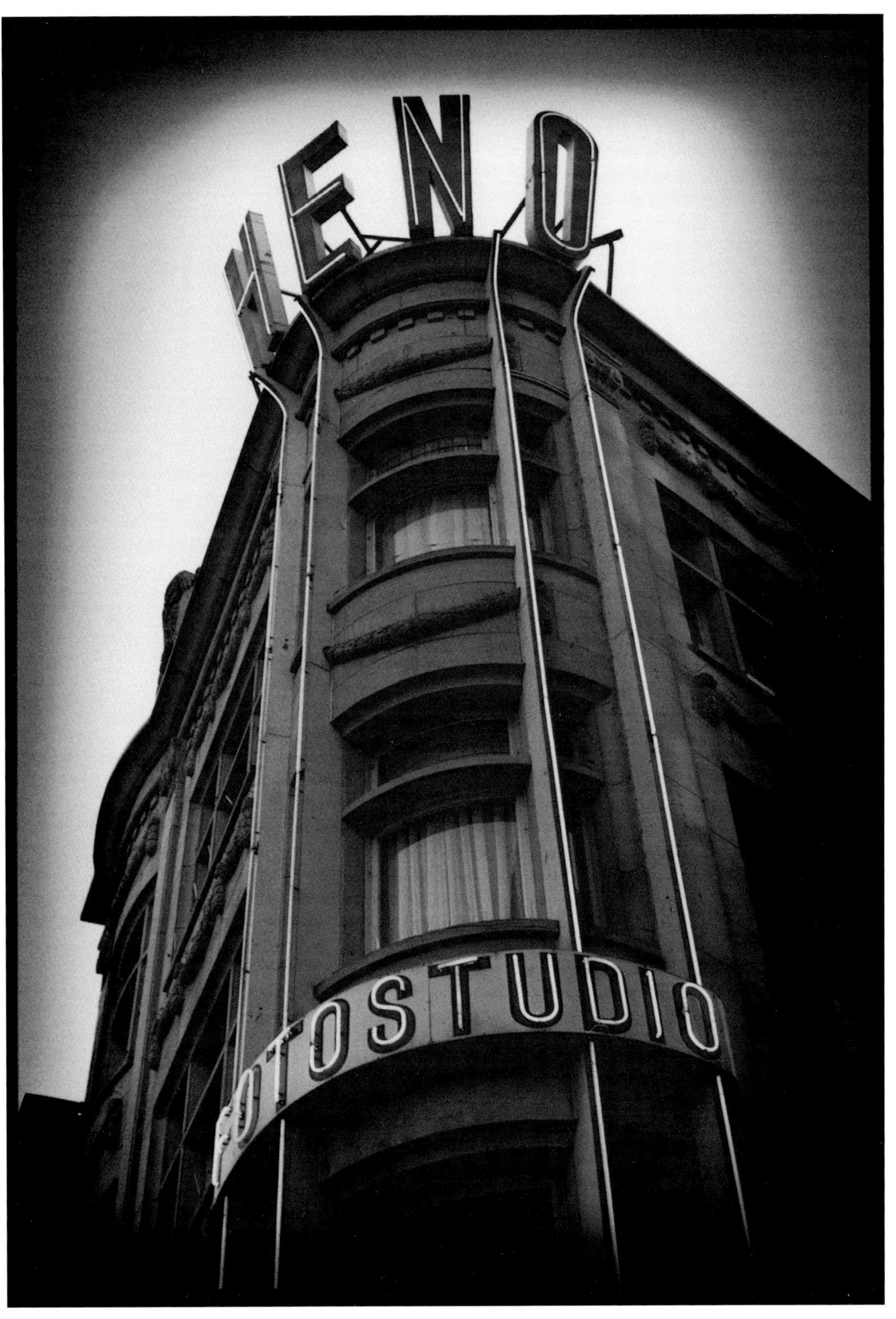
ENO
FOTOSTUDIO

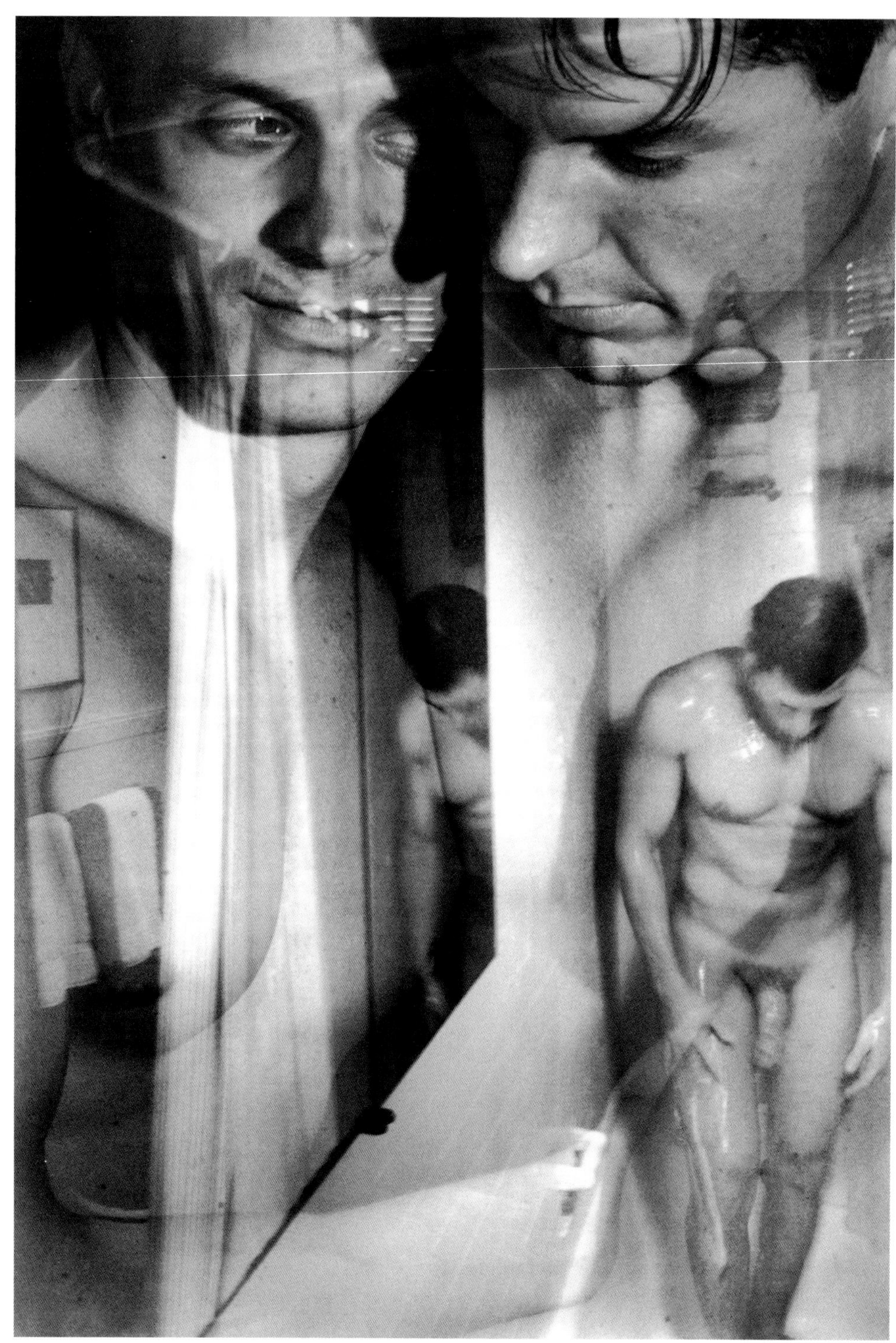

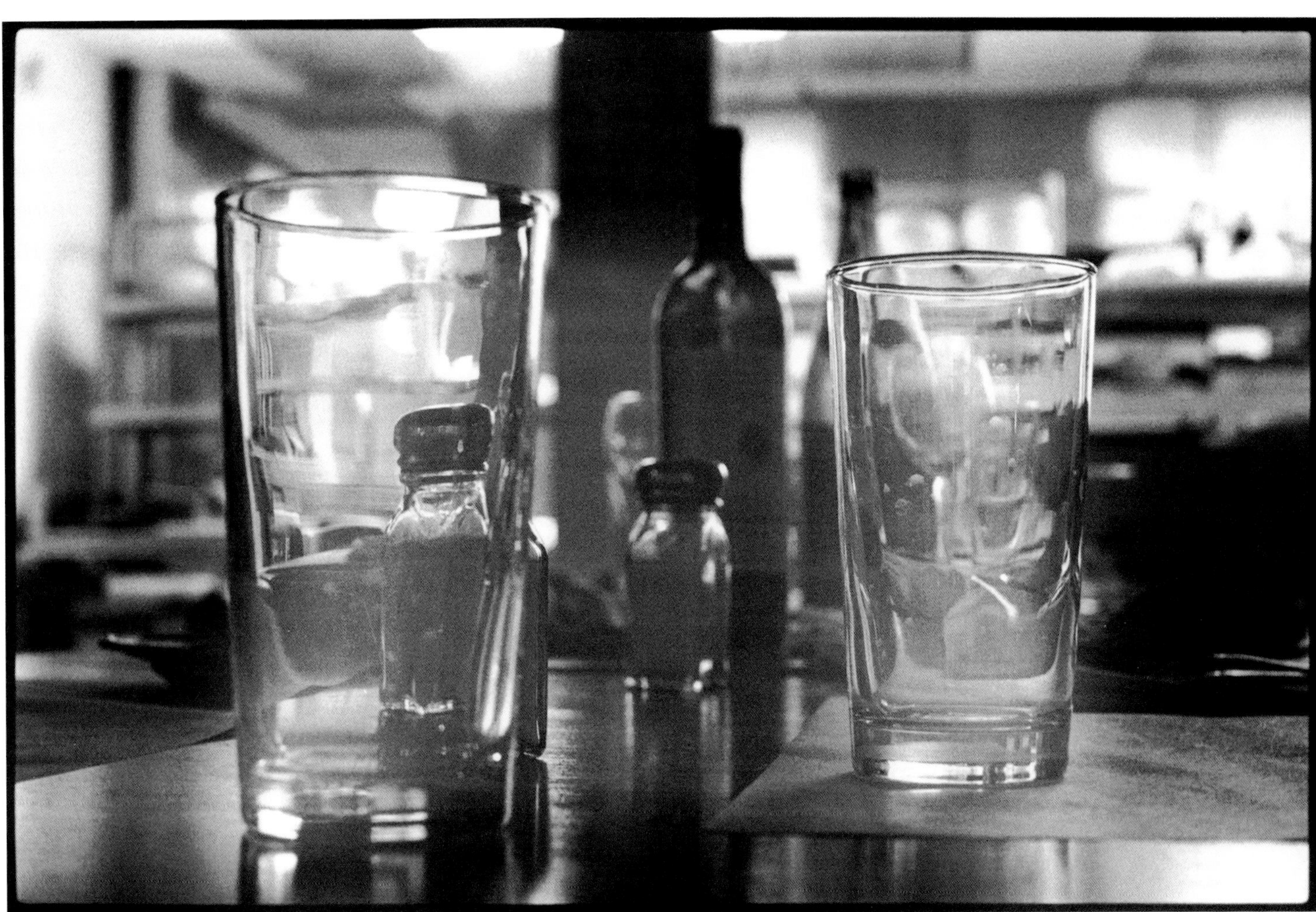

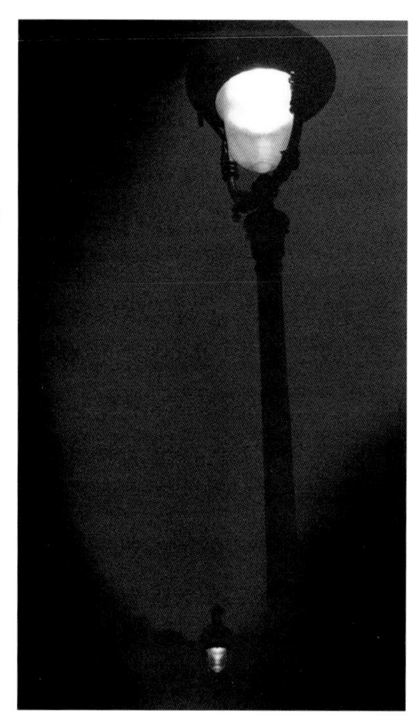
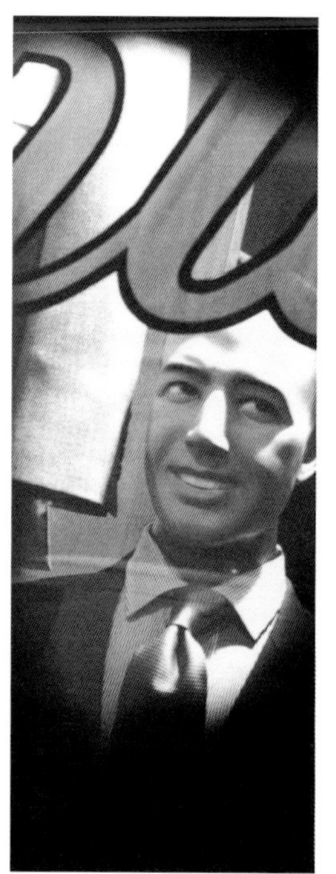
FANQUE
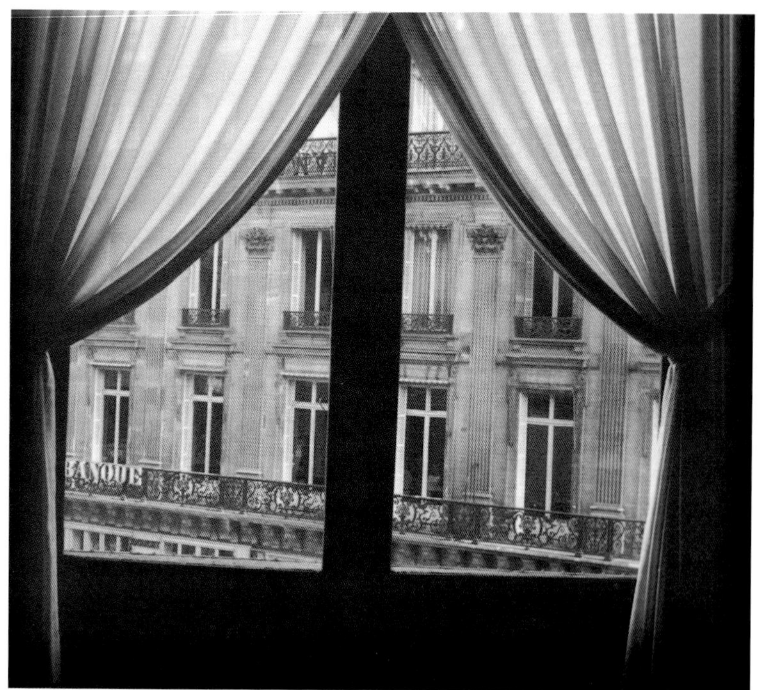

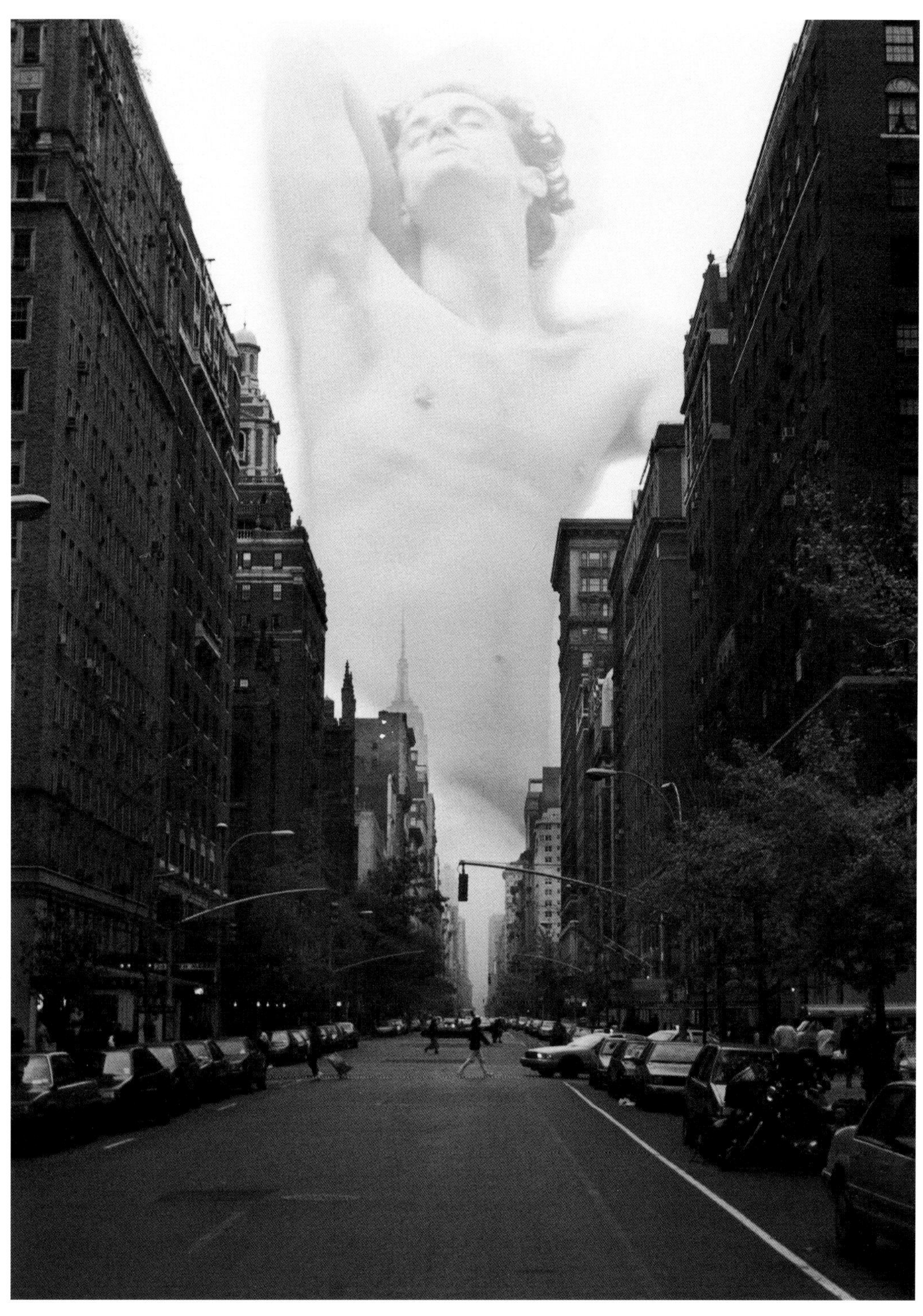

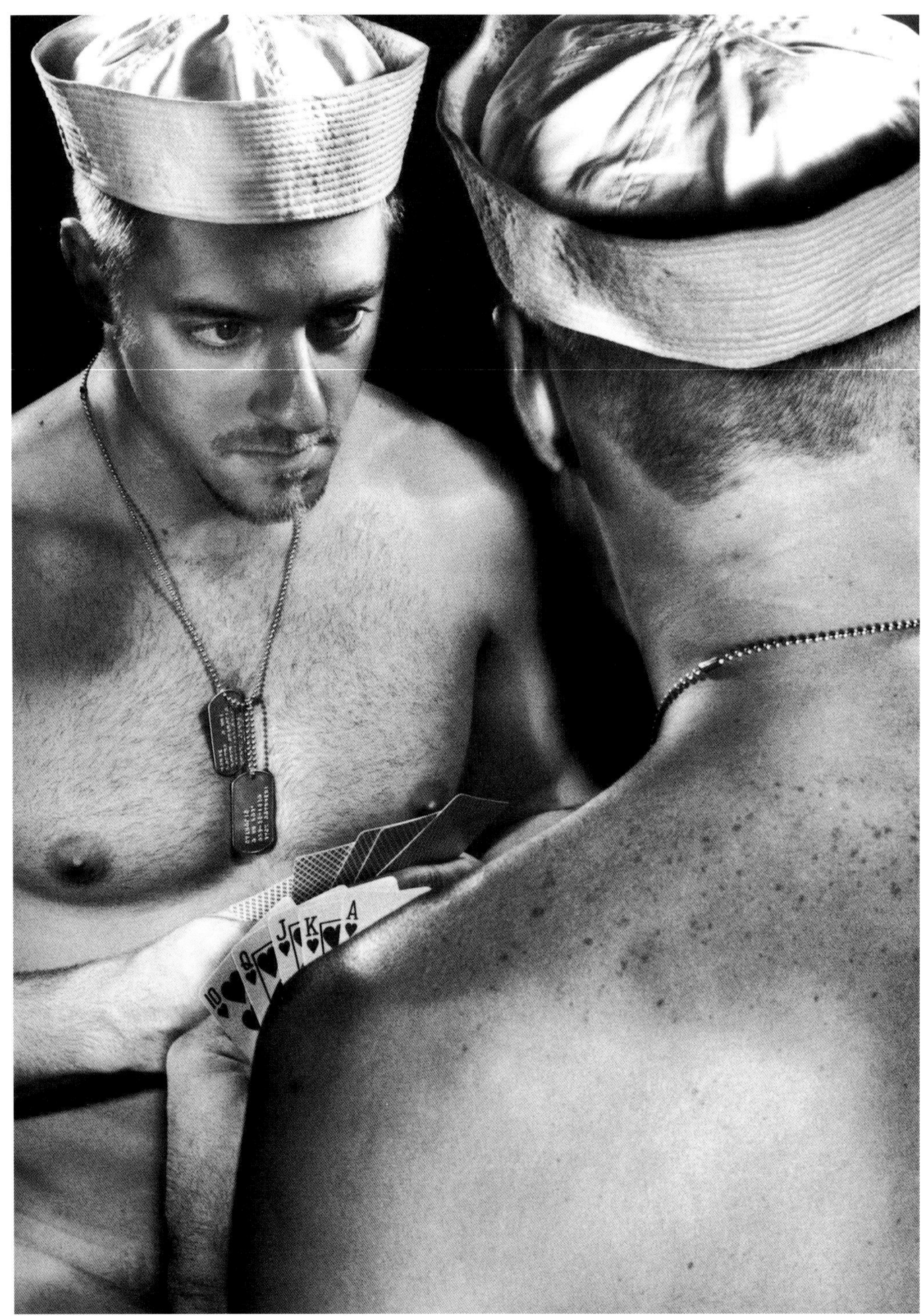

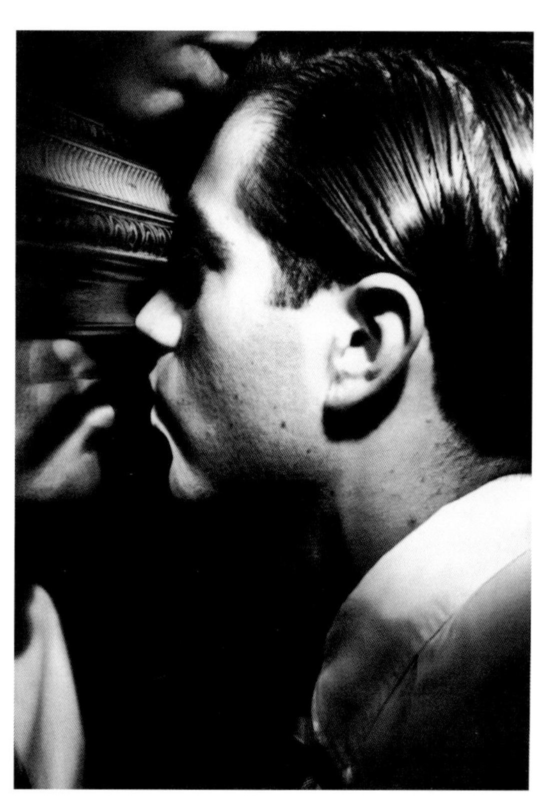

In Evening

At any rate it wouldn't have lasted long. Years
of experience make that much clear to me. But still it was a bit abrupt,
the way it all ended as Fate drew near.
The life of beauty was cut short.

But how heady our perfumed unctions were,
how exquisite the bed where we lay,
to what pleasures we gave our bodies away.

An echo of the days of pleasure,
an echo of those days passed near me,
charged with some of the fire our youth had fanned.
Again I took a letter in my hands
and read it over and over until the light had failed.

And I went out onto the balcony, melancholy —
I went so I might clear my head by seeing at least
a little of my beloved city,
some little movement in the street, and in the shops.

C. P. Cavafy

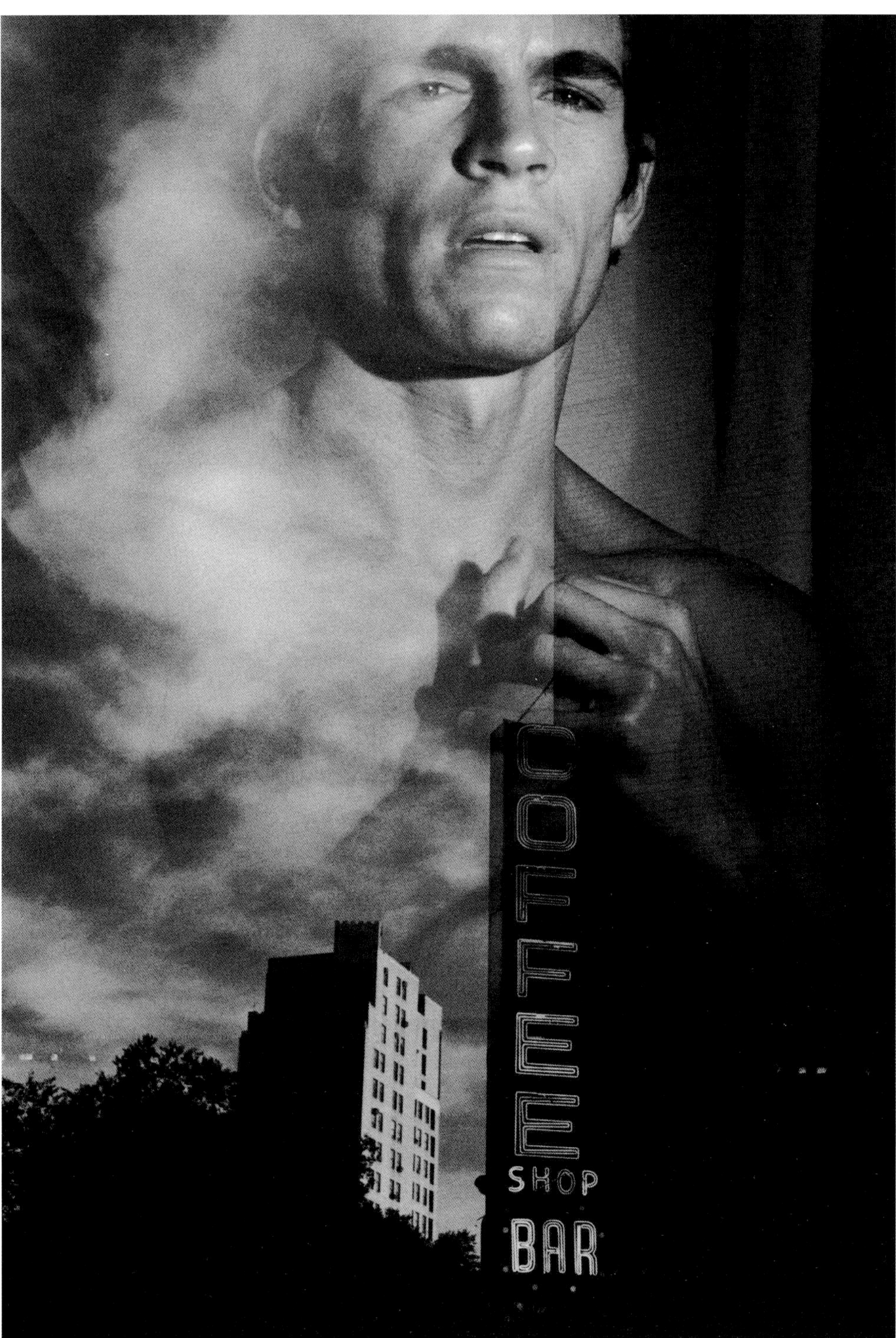

COFFEE
SHOP
BAR

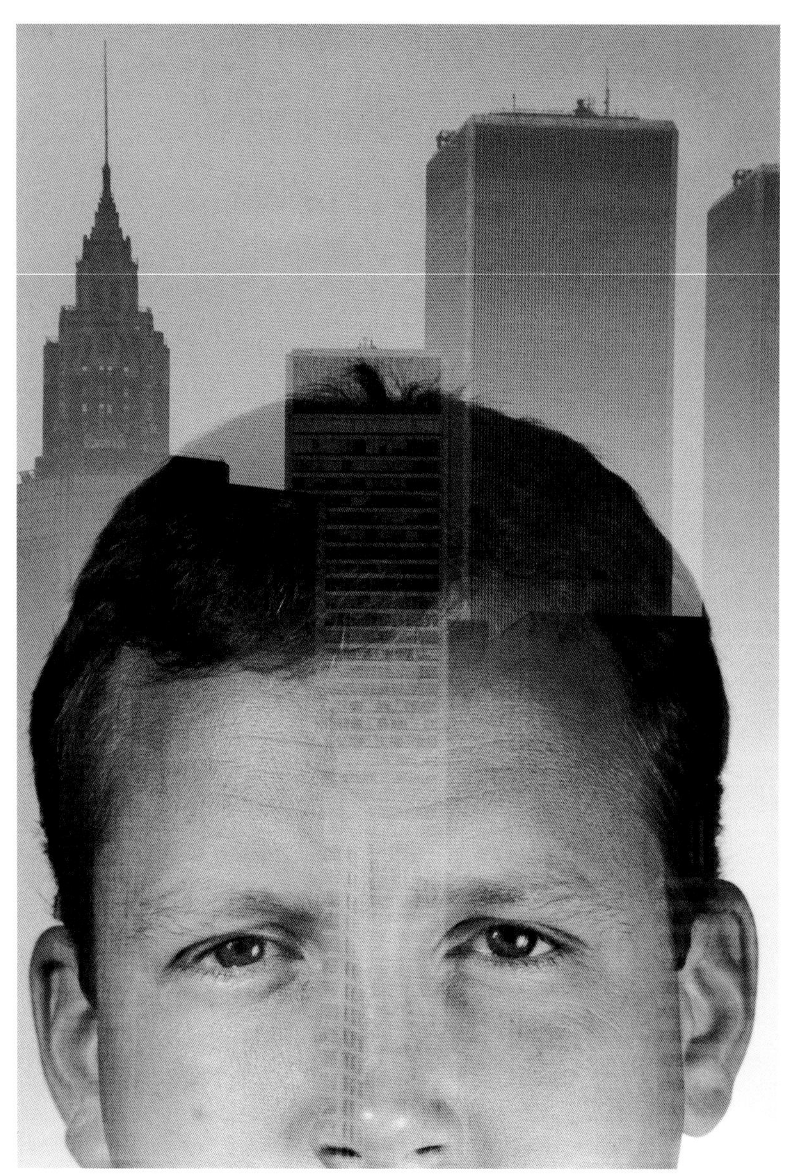

I HATE CLOWNS

A conversation with Race Willard

RW: Why do you feel it's important to combine images?

BT: My work is frequently combined with narrative poetry so it has a certain sense of a moment or an emotion that it needs to convey – I'm illustrating a feeling or a sentiment or an idea – so making a person bigger – like the one on the wall there [p.57] you become tuned into his immediate sort of feeling and you see that he's rising above the city because that's powerful and it's what the poem that that picture was designed to go with, by Cavafy – it's what it was designed to show – it's showing this guy's longing or solitude and you see that he's in the city but the city is only there to color your awareness of where he's coming from in terms of his attitude . . .

RW: But is it from him or within you?

BT: It's from within me.

RW: You show a lot of objects, solitary, like the flowers, and the table [p. 4]. What drives you to express yourself through the medium of photography?

BT: I like it because it's more flexible and fast in terms of getting something done and the fact that you can sell more than one of a certain work is good – it doesn't take a year to do one thing like a painting and then it's gone . . .

RW: Yeah, but what one has more significance to you?

BT: My paintings were always based on my photographs – the photography always came first, so I suppose that it's really the foundation for any art that I do.

RW: Why do you use montages – why is everything a montage or a collective grouping?

BT: It's a sense of wanting to tell a story with a single image . . .

RW: Well not even that – you have these groupings . . .

BT: Like a narrative sequence almost of single images . . .

RW: Does everything have the same theme to you?

BT: Many times it has similar themes – this picture [p. 21] is an illustration of three specific characters in a story – and by story I mean a narrative poem that I've written to go with the pictures – I overlap them with an exposure of the place where they're having their story unfold. In terms of everything meaning the same I think there's a sense of independence or isolation even or being alone with one's thoughts and there's an erotic edge - a sort of still eroticism . . .

RW: Your storytelling is therapeutic – do you ever do any self-portraits?

BT: There is one in here – and I don't know if I'm going to reveal that to my readership here, but . . .

RW: [laughs] Why? Too personal?

BT: I don't know – perhaps – it *is* true that I present my personality in my pictures and reflect myself in them – hence the title of the book, "Heart's Unwitting Likeness" – you're taking this thing that doesn't know – like a gate in Paris – it doesn't know that it's reflecting you, but it is, unwittingly, as a likeness of you.

RW: It's how you work through it in your head – made tangible.

BT: True! Now, you'll notice that I have a lot of central axes – there's a lot of balance and symmetry. . .

RW: Is that because you look for that in your life or that you feel you have it?

BT: Probably because I feel I have it.

RW: Do you want to show that to other people?

BT: I want to show that, exactly.

RW: Who inspires you?

BT: Well my Dad gave me the camera that I'm still using today which is actually broken at the moment . . .

RW: [laughs] They do that from time to time.

BT: I think that in terms of influences I'm inspired by André Kertész and Robert Frank and certainly Sally Mann and most of the images that inspire me are ones that have a sense of organized sensuality.

RW: So that's what inspires you.

BT: Yeah. I don't like, you know, kind of messy sensuality.

RW: What do you consider messy?

BT: Messy would be like the wrong angle or something not balanced or something kind of flying off the edge of the page, you know . . .

RW: Or people that get up late?

BT: People that get up late, yeah – that's good, I like that.

RW: That whole thing just throws you off why? 'Cause you're threatened?

BT: Because I'm seriously German. And speaking of German, here's a fabulous picture of the Siegessäule, the Victory Column in Berlin [p. 38] . . .

RW: And a clown [p. 38] – I hate clowns.

BT: You hate clowns, why?

RW: They scared me as a small child . . .

BT: They scare you, does that clown scare you?

RW: Yes.

BT: Why?

RW: Because you can't recognize him.

BT: But isn't that great make-up?

RW: It's not balanced. Does that bother you?

BT: No it doesn't – because it's part of the spontaneous nature of his appearance which -

RW: You don't really like movement – you're very still – it's that balancing – you get out of control that way . . .

BT: Uh-huh. So, what do you think is going on there [p41]?

RW: What's going on there? Umm . . . it's a wet dream.

BT: Well, you know, some people would just say it's a guy asleep. It was originally based on a short poem in French that was just talking about dreaming about someone that you loved and now it's sort of an AIDS allegory that's suggested by the Cavafy poem that's across the page from it. What do you think about AIDS-inspired art?

RW: I think if you feel something, you should do it. I don't think that you should think consciously when doing something that this is AIDS or this is a picture of a black man or racism or what not, I just think that it should come from within – I think that that's art. No, that really bothers me, those kind of things.

BT: What?

RW: Things that seem contrived, or, like this is a racist – I mean, that's probably my biggest problem with it . . .

BT: It's a moral statement or whatever, that seems sort of

belabored . . .

RW: It's commercial! And I don't think that anything of merit should . . .

BT: Hmm. Since you know her [Madonna] . . .

RW: Uh-huh . . .

BT: What did you think of the "Like A Prayer" video in that regard? Whether that was sincere or just kind of sensational? I thought the imagery was, if it was inspired in order to have great imagery, then it was sincere because the imagery was terrific.

RW: Um – I'm sorry, that's a hairy question for the simple fact that people change – and for me to make a comment on it now and what I think that it's purpose was at the time are two different things. You know what I mean? I think it had something good behind it – I also think it had something made to make money and shock and raise eyebrows. I think that . . .

BT: Do you think I'm trying to do that?

RW: No – no, no. I don't really think I see things sensational-ized in your pictures, I mean there's a sense of – I see a control factor. I see that you manipulate things – which is a form of controlling things – you like substantial things like buildings and tables and even the flowers that you choose are not delicate – it's very structured -

BT: This is a diptych [p. 42] – from the same series as the one of the three heads with Wall Street in the background and it's designed to tell a story . . .

RW: But you could definitely look into it and see a lot of things. Not just what you intended . . .

BT: Well, photographs that you remember are ones that make you think about something personal – you have your own experi-ence about them. There were a lot of success story pictures that I didn't include here because I didn't think they were as resonant . . .

RW: They were too commercial?

BT: They were too commercial – like tourist snapshots.

RW: But why do you think they were such a success?

BT: Because they record something that everyone knows about and immediately relates to in a very easy to understand, yet dynamic way.

RW: So you don't want to make it easy for people to under-stand?

BT: Well, fine art tends to be more about the emotions of the artist.

RW: I think in mastering anything you combine, you balance what is inner consciousness and a reflection of society that relates, because knowledge is nothing unless you can communicate it, to everyone, do you know what I mean? I don't ever see art as being fine art – I think it's great if everyone can look at it and take something from it – even though it has a sense of commercialism, because it's going to attract people. Like all of our icons that we look at.

BT: Certainly a piece of fine art in a gallery is designed to be commercial. At the same time a photograph in a magazine – that certainly has a sense of intuition and personal power that's conveyed by the photographer who takes the picture of that woman in the dress, wherever she is, you know?

RW: I think fashion is extremely commercial . . .

BT: But it's still a reflection of the photographer . . .

RW: I think everything you do is a reflection of yourself. The way you dress, the way you speak – why did you make a montage of this [p.44]?

BT: Most of these images are in-camera double or triple exposures – it's rare that they are sandwiches done in the darkroom.

RW: I mean here, it's like dominatrix meets Wonderland. You've made it look kind of light and airy – why? Was it too harsh without that?

BT: The lights to me mean something inside the people – their intoxication – that they are either feeling – or something they've taken, or whatever . . .

RW: [laughs] Was that a drug reference?

BT: That was a sanitized drug reference.

RW: So they're on hallucinogens, basically.

BT: They're hallucinating in an underground dungeon. And those are the same people from the story on Wall Street, you know, so let your mind run wild.

RW: Twisted individuals.

BT: It's a twisted story. This guy like kills everyone. Stay away from him.

RW: Not only is it a beautiful photograph, it offers clues to a very important murder case!

BT: That's true – now see here's a very significant . . .

RW: . . . German . . .

BT: . . . central axis [p. 45].

RW: But do you not strive to be – I mean, Germans are not particularly very liberal individuals.

BT: True. So wouldn't you say it's an interesting thing that I'm choosing to express all this stuff that's "liberal" through my art because it's more safe than doing it myself – I get everyone else to do it for me in front of my camera. Makes sense right?

RW: [laughs] Yeah, yeah.

BT: It's like I said before, orderly sensuality or whatever. It's really just an expression of myself. This is sort of religious [p. 47] . . .

RW: Actually it's the first picture I feel I see a sense of humor – it's very religious, but -

BT: What about the man with the buildings coming out of his head [p. 58]?

RW: Well, I don't see a sense of humor – I thought that was actually really dark, and maybe a struggle for you . . . I see this man's head and buildings coming out of it – it's a problem – it's a huge weight in your head . . .

BT: So here's – again a very organized view of a photography building in Amsterdam [p. 49] – the signage is a big deal here – why do you think I like signs and letters so much?

RW: They tell you what to do.

BT: Oh really? That's good . . . well, they're pretty – letters are pretty.

RW: No . . .

BT: The picture of the two glasses through the window in Miami [p. 51]. How do you feel about it if I don't tell you anything about it – I mean does it suggest a story or anything to you?

RW: Once again, even though it's not, it looks like a montage because you see things through other things.

BT: Totally cool. Here we have more signs in the city and the people all together [p. 24] and it's sensual and remote . . .

RW: The lights again . . .

BT: The lights, yeah.

RW: Are you looking for a light?

Race Willard resists classification. He is, however, uniquely accomplished as a photographer and model of fashion. His work has appeared in *Harper's Bazaar*, *Glamour* and *Elle*. He is a resident of the planet.

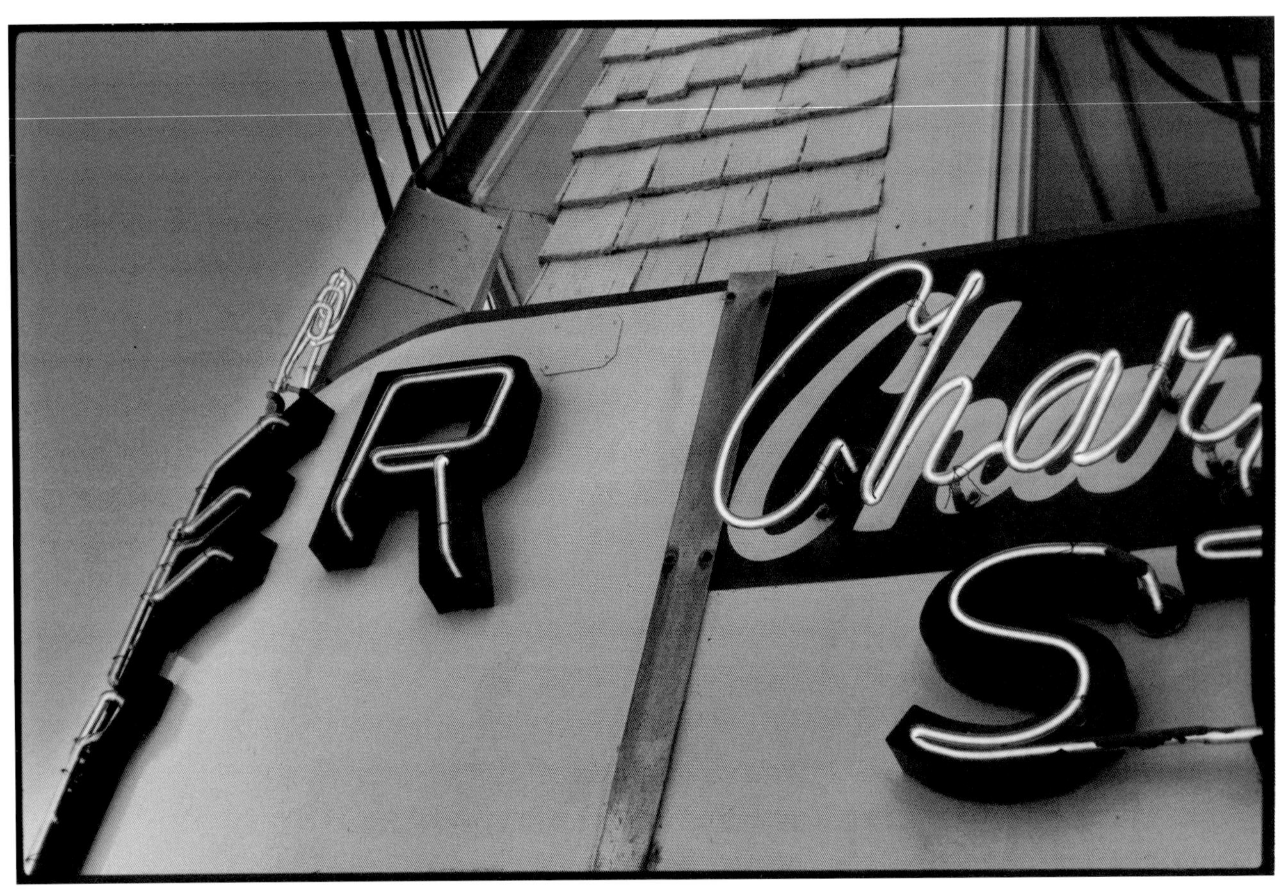
R
Char
S

P H O T O G R A P H S

Measurements in inches; height precedes width

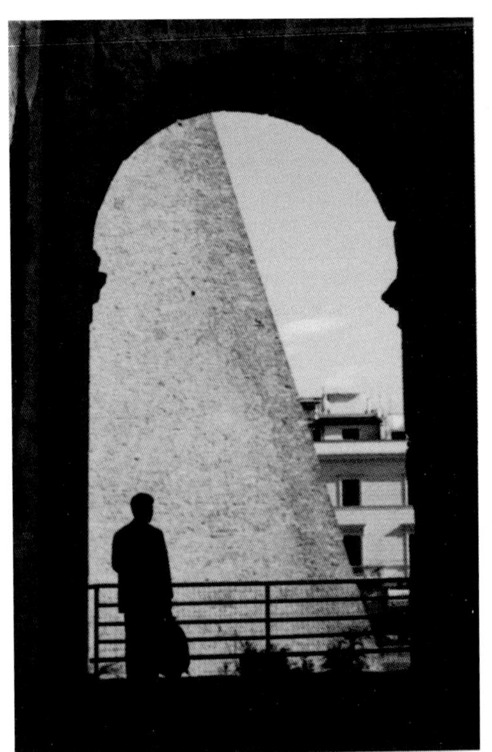

FOR

GRAY